True Karate Dō

Jeffrey Brooks

Copyright © 2019-2023 Jeffrey M. Brooks
All Rights Reserved
ISBN 979-8-218-18134-5
Pinnacle Mountain Press

Dedication

To the practitioners of Yamabayashi Ryu.

With Gratitude

to Michael Lushington, Philip Zaleski
and Tarleton Brooks,
for their generosity, insight and inspiration.

Table of Contents

Introduction ·· i
Preface ·· vii
Note ·· xiv

Part One - True Karate Dō ····················· 1
1. Damatte Keiko
2. Sakiyama Sogen's Last Letter
3. True Karate Dō
4. Sakiyama's Final Challenge
5. What Sakiyama Saw

Part Two - Approaching Kensho ············· 48
1. Intro
2. Mushin and the Science of Flow
3. Zen Culture of Zen Budo
4. Zen Budo grows from Zen Culture
5. The Path of Seeing

Doctrines of Liberation
  With senses engaged
  The human buddha becomes the transcendent buddha
  The Early Buddhist Approach

The Zen we Met
6. Ansei Ueshiro's Nin Tai
7. Satisfaction on an Autumn Evening

Part Three – Form ································169
1. Kata
2. A Different Ken Zen
3. Renzoku
4. Balance in Space Time and Mind
5. Stable Equilibrium
6. The Lost Art of the Frozen Hunter
7. Naihanchi's Strange Omission
8. One Unique Technique
9. Mindfulness in Kata

Part Four - War ································230
1. Bun Bu Ryo Do
2. Killing People and Taking Their Stuff
3. From Buddha to OODA
4. Karate and Nuclear War
5. Making History

Conclusion ································300

Part Five - Yamabayashi Ryu ················312
1. The Best Martial Art
2. Empty Hand vs Gun
3. Three instructor stages
4. Just Not the Same

5. Concealed in Kihon
6. Resistance is Futile
7. No Menkyo Kaiden
8. Dō as Jitsu
9. Play, Work, War
10. Penetrating the Truth
11. Breaking Good
12. Empty Hand vs. Drugs
13. Sweet Dreams
14. The Moment of Truth
15. The Momentum of Truth
16. The Benevolence of the Butcher
17. Kansha
18. Defense against Violence and Decadence
19. The Fog of Peace

Appendix One – Zen Doctrines of Enlightenment **380**

Appendix Two – Technical Analysis of Kata ······**399**

Glossary ···**435**

Author Bio ···**452**

Introduction

The time to decide what your life is worth is now. If you wait it will be too late. The world is changing. Everyone knows it. We try to stay on familiar ground. We try to orient like we always have. We hope the world we knew will come back. It wasn't perfect. But there was good in it.

People are making decisions that affect all of us. In sleek glass towers, in engineered caverns, on wide green campuses, every day and all night long, every night, reams of code are pouring across the global net, like lava from a volcano whose time has finally come.

It is not nature. People are doing this. People who know they are not like "the population." They are different. They are better. They get the good stuff. They know the code. They'll own the globe. The population is irrelevant.

The population knows nothing, does nothing, is clueless, useless and worthless. To be herded and farmed, tapped for wealth, drained of life.

This eager cadre, always in gear, who aspire to own everything, seems to know nothing. They are not educated in the possibilities of the human mind or body. No bioengineered chimera, no transfusion of tweaked young plasma, will fix that. They have not been briefed on the results of what they do, the consequences of a craving heart or a heartless mind.

They understand machines. They understand how machines can be taught to penetrate every moment, every place, every thought and feeling, to excavate the past and reach the future. They live the ethos of machines, murmuring the mantra of machines: more, better, faster. 24/7. It started as a rumble, it ratcheted up to a roar, now it's all you can hear. They are sure that by linking the right people at the right conferences with the right tabletop exercises, they will master disease and the tricks of nuclear war before the lights of the world go out.

They are masters of artificial intelligence, at a time when what is needed most is natural intelligence.

True Karate Dō

This book is about what can be done to keep our lives our own.

Karate may seem an unlikely way to do that. What I will show in this book is an unusual way to use it. Some aspects of this material are completely new. Some are timeless. Because of both it works, it is revolutionary, and it is needed.

The book contains new insights in technique, showing dimensions of karate which have been missed. It shows a new approach to deep transformation through practice which has been a staple of the mystique of east Asian martial arts but which was unable to deliver on its promise. I believe I can show why, and what to do to fix that.

This book is written mainly for the people who practice Yamabayashi Ryu, the Mountain Forest stream of karate. It is relevant to you because you may want to use it now, or refer to it when you are ready to take some of the steps I am describing.

Others who practice Shorin Ryu can apply this material directly.

People who practice any martial art or who are devoted to any demanding pursuit, will find this material relevant – less in the technical sections, but certainly with regard to what happens when we seek out and accept challenges which continually deepen our insight, broaden our experience, and increase our ability, for as long as we live.

The title <u>True Karate Dō</u> does not mean that I teach true karate and other people don't. It points to the aim of the book, which is to define what true karate dō might be. You may already be doing it. Excellent. This book may help clarify and deepen what you do.

The title <u>True Karate Dō</u> was given to a short piece that I wrote, an outline of my vision of karate. The title was given by Zen Master Sogen Sakiyama, Roshi, of Shuri, Okinawa, Japan, to my essay. Because he felt so strongly about its message Sakiyama Roshi translated what I wrote into Japanese, and circulated it in the karate community on Okinawa and to his students and followers abroad.

Sakiyama Sogen, Roshi

I did not use the title <u>True Karate Dō</u> for that piece. I would not have done it. But in light of Sakiyama's life of accomplishment, his global stature, and his influence as the leading proponent of Zen-budo on Okinawa, I accepted his imprimatur with gratitude. That little essay was written long ago, as I imagined what real karate could be. I pursued that path. This book outlines the results.

Preface

There are three strands of discovery woven together in my karate and they are woven together in this book. I worked on them as one project.

One was to discover the underlying technical function and fighting applications of kata. The second was the investigation of the soteriological claim, axiomatic throughout Japanese Zen-influenced budo, of the potential for ultimate liberation through martial arts practice.
The third was how to live a coherent, healthy, virtuous and worthy life through practice. All of those qualities seemed elusive, so the promise of a method was appealing.

Strand One - to discover the underlying technical function and fighting application of kata:

This information was not transmitted with the kata. It seems incomprehensible that the people who presented the kata did not know the meaning of the moves they were teaching. They would guess, make things up or try to interpret them through boxing. Sometimes they would shut down questions, tell inquiring students to just do the katas a lot and then, under pressure, you will somehow be able to make effective use of the techniques you have been practicing. None of that was valid.

The combative skills, tactics and the methods used to inculcate them in practitioners did remain encoded in the kata. The movements of the kata themselves were transmitted to us clearly enough to allow us to examine them and eventually reverse engineer them, and rediscover their meaning. The process continues.

To do this requires broad technical knowledge and some combative experience. To apply that knowledge and experience intelligently in investigation you need to be intimately familiar with the movement itself. It is not possible to properly interpret kata using only experience in the dojo and in competition.

My experience in law enforcement was helpful in this regard, drawing on my interactions with violent people, armed and unarmed, in criminal investigations, and as an instructor of law enforcement defensive tactics, firearms and use of force. Members of our Yamabayashi Ryu karate group, friends and colleagues, and others with combative experience in the military and law enforcement, have contributed their insights and expertise as well.

I went outside our style and looked at how people, trained and untrained, defend themselves, and how they attack. In addition to personal experience,

I drew on recordings and recollections of encounters, and by observing and participating in martial arts and professional combative training which makes use of throwing, grappling, ground fighting, precision targeting, seizing, breath and energy cultivation, body and mind conditioning, and energy flow.
I traveled widely to see what interesting instructors were showing, and to see what I could learn that might illuminate hidden dimensions of our kata.

All that time I practiced every day. In my investigation of the purposes of the movements in our kata, searching for practical application, I never deviated from the movement of our kata. I went on the assumption that the surface movements and technique sequences had been retained intact, but that the understanding of them, the way to actually use them, had not. This assumption proved useful.

What I am referring to as "our kata" are the eighteen Okinawan karate kata grouped together by Shoshin Nagamine, founder of Matsubayashi Ryu to form the curriculum of his style. These kata form the foundation of Yamabayashi Ryu. I practiced these continually and examined them – looking for ways to understand every move in every kata as a tool to train combat-effective self-defense. I explain this approach and my rationale in this book.

Strand Two has been the investigation of the soteriological claim, axiomatic throughout Japanese Zen-influenced budo and other east Asian martial traditions, of the potential for ultimate liberation through martial arts practice. I tell something about how I did the search, who I studied with, what material I drew from and what I discovered. It is new, iconoclastic, liberating and extremely useful. As I began my search, I was idealistic, credulous and naïve. Which was good. Although it led to some difficulties, it allowed me a passionate commitment to practice, a devotion to moving, training, searching and learning which I would not have had had I been cynical or tentative about my faith in the promise of budo, or the efficacy of the method described within the traditions for achieving it.

My early karate teachers didn't know too much about this, so I went to visit a number of Zen and karate teachers, and other experts in the US and in Japan. Historically Zen was not closely associated with Okinawa or with Okinawan karate, but I found a strong connection with the leading Zen teacher on Okinawa, Sogen Sakiyama, Roshi. He was an extraordinary karate practitioner as well. Sakiyama Roshi was a direct student of Miyagi Chojun, founder of Goju Ryu. He was the Zen teacher of Shoshin Nagamine.

True Karate Dō

It was Shoshin Nagamine who introduced me to Zen meditation at his dojo in Naha, and this made the introduction to Sakiyama Roshi quite natural. I also spent time at American Zen temples and centers.

I had the opportunity to meet with several accomplished western scholars and Tibetan teachers of Tibetan Buddhism, including the eminent practitioner and author Tulku Thondup. He kindly took time on several occasions to give me valuable insights and instruction. He made a number of suggestions for further exploration and practice. Although I was familiar with his books, his ideas and his recommendation for practice, I was not able to put what he wrote to work until I met with him for face-to-face instruction and guidance. That experience informs the way I present the advanced practice material in this book. Most significantly, I have had a chance to study in the thorough and lucid work of Bhikkhu Bodhi, American monk, translator and author, and of Bhikkhu Analayo, German scholar-practitioner and teacher, both of the Theravada tradition. In addition to these teachers, writer, scholar and practitioner Philip Zaleski has been so generous with his time and mind, giving me access to people, ideas and perspectives from worlds beyond my experience.

As I traveled, trained and studied, the shortcomings of the conventions of contemporary life, and of our response to east Asian martial and religious cultures, became clear. Unwholesome modes of behavior were accepted, even encouraged. Values, taken for granted as right and advanced, turned out to be pathological and confused. This was reflected in cultural life, social life, and dojo life. As I trained with honest, dedicated people the remedy also became clear.

Strand Three of the investigation: By incorporating the ideals of personal conduct and the intentional training of character, as described in the traditions, within the framework of the dojo, it was possible to approach a coherent, healthy, virtuous and worthy way of life. It was clear that this is to be done through practice. Not by importing extras, or talking about good ideas, but by living in a way that is honest, vigorous and generous. By training in a way that orients our lives to meaning and purpose. How to do that, and how to conform our understanding, conduct, and frame of mind to this standard, was the task. It led to a reframing of some key elements of training, and reuniting several streams of knowledge which were separated long ago. I report on the discoveries and their use in this book.

These three strands are distinct, but they are not separate. Like a strong rope they are intertwined at every point. They appear together in the book. The philosophy and the kata analysis which are most technical are collected in the two appendixes at the end. Relevant video is posted on our website.

Throughout my exploration, underlying all the variety in cultures, ideas, personalities, and values, one constant was my daily practice of karate. Moving, alone or with others, with a clear mind and as much skill as I could muster, was my main interest from day one. It remains so.

Note

A question dojo members and visitors often ask is: "Did you ever really use it?"

I tell them there were times when I was young when I lived in violent places, where robberies and muggings were part of life every day, and that there were times when I did rely on physical skills.

I tell them that in my law enforcement career there were encounters with violent people which required a physical response. That the judicious use of force in defense of innocent, victimized or exploited people, is good and necessary. In a way it even benefits the robber, thief, assailant or murderer, by preventing them from collecting the consequences of doing even more harm. I have stories, as everyone does.

There were times when I was dealing with people who were accustomed to a degree of brutality which is unfamiliar to most of us here. Times when people attempted intimidation and submission. Times when I needed sustained attention for hours in places where I could not afford to tune out for even a second. And so on. My training helped with all of that.

That seems to give people confidence that I might be a reliable source of information about self-defense.

What I would prefer to tell them is that I use my training every day and all the time. You have your body with you, you have your mind with you, wherever you are. If you are under pressure or busy you use them well.

If you have a lull, you can always train. No one can tell that is what you are doing. It is not a big deal. You just draw your attention wherever you want it and train. That's one of the ways I use it.

That is not the answer that people are looking for. If I answered that way it would sound evasive or strange. But it is true. If I know people long enough, I tell them that. If they train for long enough, they find out for themselves.

***

Part One
True Karate Dō

Damatte Keiko

It was a short drive from the dojo to the beach – on Okinawa you are always close to the ocean. The driver was a long-time karate practitioner who agreed to teach me a new kata during the last few days of my visit.

The stretch of beach he chose was wide-open, with the endless sea, brilliant sun, and a constant tropical breeze to keep us cool. There was nothing formal about the training, no dojo etiquette or anything. We just began: He moved. I copied.

There I was, following his kata as best I could, watching his turns and techniques, trying to take it all in, adjusting my hands, changing feet – doing what we all do when we try to copy a new kata for the first time.

He would demonstrate. I would imitate. He would say "Ko yatte!" And then demonstrate the move. I would copy. He would move my arm, push my shoulder or kick my leg. Then he would do the move again, and say "Ko yatte."

I was not familiar with this expression. Was it an ancient Okinawan mantra with the power to convey the mystic secrets of karate?

"Ko yatte" means "Like this." "Do it like this!"

It was an easy way to learn. Very efficient. Without any verbal description of the steps or analysis of the techniques, I learned the embusen of that kata in about an hour. The lack of a shared language was not a barrier to instruction, it facilitated instruction. I noticed it right away.

Back home some instructors would go on and on, explaining details of the techniques, searching for just the right words, explaining the tips they had picked up from their teachers over the years, trying to help us learn. We stood and listened. It was hard to remember all the details. We were not much better at the end of the explanation than we were at the beginning, maybe a little worse, because we spent precious training time listening instead of practicing.

A tip, a precise pointer, directed to a particular individual at just the right time, can be very helpful. But mainly we learn by moving. We refine and discover as we go.

Damatte Keiko is a good approach: "Don't talk – Just train."

We had a floor to ceiling mural of this expression, which hung in our dojo for many years. My wife Tarleton painted it. People liked it, so we made little prints of it, and they appeared in many dojos around the world. I used to see them around when I travelled. It is a good reminder.

Damatte Keiko, mural by Tarleton Brooks

At first, we use "Damatte Keiko" to create conditions for efficient training. That is step one. There is a more profound reason to use this principle. It opens the door to deep accomplishment in martial arts. It is accessible to everyone who wants it. But some martial artists do not get a chance to use this because they are not aware of it, or have not understood it clearly enough to put it into action.

Focused training, unmediated by language, pauses, or distractions, is the way to produce the essential "phase transformation" that leads to mastery.

If you do not use it, you will not master your art. No matter how sound your lineage, how prestigious your system, how great your teacher, how much kata or kumite you have done, how many applications you know, as valuable as they are they are not sufficient to fulfill our potential or the potential of our practice. To reach that potential we have to cross a phase boundary.

Phase transformation in thermodynamics refers to the change in the properties of a material as a result of changes in temperature and pressure. Ice turns to water. Water turns to vapor. Those are phase transformations.

The temperature of the water may change slowly. But the phase change is sudden. Ice will be ice at -100° and at -50° and at 32°. But go one degree higher and it will melt, it will become water. Same chemistry. Different properties. If we continue to raise the temperature, the water will feel warm and then hot but it will still be water. Until it reaches its boiling point. Then it will hit its phase boundary and vaporize. Same material. Different properties.

Karate practitioners undergo analogous phase transformations after enough time in the heat and pressure of training. The addition of the heat and pressure of training is gradual and cumulative. The transformation can be sudden.

This is referenced extensively in east Asian martial arts lore and literature. The most well-known texts in the medieval Japanese budo tradition hint at it. Some explain it. These texts have been well-translated. But the ideas too rarely make their way into practice.

The phase transformation of karate practitioners is produced by training under periodic, incremental increases of heat and pressure. Similar to the crafting of the blade of a samurai sword. By undergoing this process, the practitioner changes: he or she does not just acquire more skill. Their body, mind and life have new properties. They are transformed.

If the training is not intense enough to bring the practitioner to a high-energy state, then there will be inadequate heat and pressure even to begin the process. If the energy of training is not intensified and continuously re-applied then the practitioner will not reach the phase boundary.

If the cooling-off period between trainings is longer than needed for recovery then the heat, and the practitioner's skills, will dissipate. They will have to restart the process or remain at a skill-plateau. In that case, despite "years" of training, he or she will not approach the phase boundary. Some may fantasize about mastery, wish for mastery, feel sure they have put in enough dojo training-hours to deserve mastery, but they will not be able to achieve it. Funakoshi Gichin was an Okinawan teacher of Shorin Ryu karate. He was instrumental in introducing Okinawan karate to Japan in the 1920's. His karate technique has global influence through his organization and its branch styles. His first manual of his kata and theory, the Karate-Do Kyohan, is a key source for Japanese karate around the world.

In the Karate-Do Kyohan, Funakoshi compared consistent training to the "tea kettle remaining on the fire." He did not elaborate. This is understood as encouragement to keep at it. But there is a deeper implication which is essential for advanced achievement.

If our training is calibrated to raise the heat (the intensity of the training) and pressure (the performance demand) high enough to affect the phase transformation, and skillfully enough so as not to injure the practitioner, and if it is repeated along a proper gradient of frequency and intensity of practice, the practitioner will transform.

In the traditional craftsmanship of a samurai sword multiple alloys are laminated and different parts of the blade are tempered under different conditions, to produce a suite of qualities that none of the components have on their own. And there is a deeper transformation: heat and pressure produce a new crystalline structure within the finished metal. This makes a weapon with strength, flexibility, hardness and resilience far exceeding the qualities of the raw materials. And those qualities will remain present in the weapon after the heat and pressure applied during fabrication are withdrawn.

Reaching phase transformations in martial arts practice is rare and difficult but it is doable. It is what the old texts are talking about. Setting aside obstructions to training – avoiding unnecessary talk and thinking, disengaging from irrelevant sights and sounds in your environment, feelings in your body or mind, and focusing your attention, will and skill on the moment of action – are necessary. That was what circumstances required me to do on the beach that day on Okinawa long ago.

I will outline where the first martial arts phase boundary is, how practitioners approach it, and how to use this for deep training. To make the approach we "Don't talk, just train."

***

Sakiyama Sogen's Last Letter

Shortly after I last saw him, Sakiyama Sogen, Roshi of Kozenji Zendo, Shuri, Okinawa communicated his understanding of karate to me. This is an excerpt from his letter:

"Dear Mr. Brooks,
Today many karate students, particularly karate teachers, neither know the difference between karate

and karate-do, nor do they try to discover the difference. This I regret very much. True karate-do can be learned only when we have realized the mysteries of our heart and mind, and realized the mysteries of our body with all our heart and mind and strength. Otherwise, karate will be nothing more than a little game, a way to show off. Ultimately it will degenerate into contests or street fighting. It is a shame.

"The essentials of karate-do can only be attained through profound practice. This means that in order to realize what is essential we must experience deep samadhi. I am sure you fully understand what I am trying to say. It is most important for us, and for the younger generations, that we cultivate our heart and mind.

"The final hurdle for us is to be free from the limitations of our own ego. The disease of modern people is that they are slaves to money, power, fame, etc. They are enslaved by their own egos, and are unaware of it. You will become a true master when you become aware of it, and become free of it. There is no easy way, but it is the most important task, one worth devoting one's life to accomplishing. This is the central task for anyone trying to master a true martial art.

"As I am writing to you, I can vividly feel your sincerity and passion to pursue this and to master karate-do. 'Do' is an endless and severe way. Therefore, we must endlessly exert ourselves to attain it. How wonderful the 'Do' is!"

Sincerely yours,

Sogen Sakiyama

***

True Karate Dō

Sakiyama Roshi wrote a long letter to me after I visited him at his Zen temple in Shuri, Okinawa, near the towering stone walls of the royal castle of the old Ryukyuan Kingdom.

Earlier, I had written a brief essay, which I sent to him. In it I described what I believed to be the essential moral foundation and high spiritual aspiration which are necessary to fulfill the hidden potential of karate. He had been an accomplished karate practitioner, steeped in the tradition's culture and methods. The approach I suggested was different from any I had encountered. I hoped he would understand the implications of my message.

I was quite surprised to find that Sakiyama Roshi had translated my short essay into Japanese and circulated it, via the media and personally, among the karate community in Okinawa. The main part of the essay is a list of the "Six Perfections," a traditional set of six paths of action to be taken by spiritual aspirants. My essay begins with brief presentation of our predicament, and suggests how dojo practice, along the lines of this approach, is relevant to resolving it.

In Japanese Sakiyama Roshi named my essay "真の空手道", True Karate Dō.

Here is what I wrote:

Many people feel they are missing their lives, that real life is going on somewhere out there. To fix this feeling they seek excitement, diversion, power, money, contention, or sink into passivity, waiting for the weekend, waiting for their ship to come in, or for their fortunes to change. But none of these strategies will relieve the deep feeling that something is missing.

Family, work, friends, community are all parts of the picture. But one way to help remedy this feeling of disorientation and emptiness is dedication to a life of practice aimed at perfection.

The perfection we aim at in karate begins as a striving for perfection of technique. We focus our efforts on unifying our mind and body, bringing them under our control.

As we practice over weeks, months and years, our bodies grow stronger, more flexible, healthier. We overcome fear. Our minds become more focused. Our will becomes more resilient. Our emotions become more stable. We breathe more deeply. The flow of energy through our bodies becomes more harmonious.

Through relentless technical polishing we can manifest a deeper perfection. But our minds must be tuned toward it.

Traditionally this is called "perfection of wisdom" and is practiced by means of six elements. We use these elements in practice.

真の空手道

多くの人々は人生を空しいものと感じ、生きがいを実感することができずにいる。この虚無感を充たそうと、人々は地位、権力、金、名声、等々の刺激を求め、又は、無気力に沈み、何者かがこの虚無感を充たそうと、人々は地位、権力、金、名声、等々の刺激を求め、又は、いずれの手段を用いようとも、この虚無感を救うことはできない。それを救う唯一の道は絶対の真理を目指しての修行に打ち込むことである。

空手において我々が目指す真なるものとは、技の完成にむけて努力することから始まる。我々は、意識を集中し心身をコントロールせんとする。
絶えざる修業の反復により、我々の身体はより強くなり、より素敏になり、より健康になる。我々は、恐怖を克服し、精神は集中力を増す。我々の意志はより活力を増す。我々の感情はさらに安定する。我々の呼吸は更に深くなる。我々の身体を通して流れるエネルギーは高度の調和を示す。

厳しい技の鍛錬を通して我々は、より深い真理に到達する。但し、我々の心もこれに調和しなければならない。仏教の伝統的表現では、この状態を"知恵の完成"と呼び、6通りの行を用いて修行することになる。我々は空手の修行において、この6法を用いる。

布施 ‥‥ 布施とは、他人に対して寛大な態度をとること。寛大な態度とは、我々の知識、親切心、エネ
(奉仕)　　ルギーを、他人に対して惜しみなく与えることである。

持戒 ‥‥ "持戒"という言葉は時代遅れの響きを持っているように感じるかも知れない。又、何か抑圧
(道義)　　的な、制約的なものと、聞こえるかも知れない。我々の修行においては、それは解放を意味する。自戒と言う言葉は我々にとって、他人を搾取しないこと、金、権力、性、名声、等々の為に他人を利用しないこと、を意味する。
他人を尊敬することにより、我々は、修行の為の望ましい環境を作り、そして、我々自身と他人を、寄立ちや対立でかき乱されることから解放する。

精進 ‥‥ 善人であるだけでは十分ではない。強さ、有能さ、要領の良さだけでも十分ではない。
(努力)　　我々は、貴重な、一身体、心、知力一を授かっている。我々が授かったこの貴重な資質は、それを十分に認識し、活用した時にのみ、我々自身と他人の為に生かすことができる。
それには、耐えざる精進が必要であり、どうでもいい事で心を取り乱さないこと、気まぐれ、自己満足、自己中心的怒然の頑なさ、等々の我々の有意義であるべき修行、又は他の全ての修行を妨害するものに捕らわれないことが必要である。

忍辱 ‥‥ この言葉は積極的な意味での忍耐を意味する。一一一それは繰り返し我々が直面する避けがた
(忍耐)　　い障害に負けずに修行を続ける為に必要な忍耐を意味する。それは、困難に耐えんとする意志力であり、耐えざる修行に打ち込もうとする、意志力である。

禅定 ‥‥ 瞑想とは、畳に坐っての瞑想とか特定の宗派の修行方法のみを意味するものではない。瞑想と
(瞑想)　　は、我々のすべての行為、すべての思考、すべての言葉に心がこもっていることである。それは心を整える修行であり、そこから、我々自身の本質、我々の宇宙の本質に対する洞察が生まれてくる。

知恵 ‥‥ 六番目の要素は知恵である。知恵はこれまで述べた諸修行の頂点である。
真なるものを目指しての修行、我々にとって空手はその為の行である。行を通して我々は充実した人生を送ることができる。絶えざる技の探究の中で、我々はより深く、更に深くなっていく。しかし、絶えざる技の修練は必要であるがそれだけでは空手の本質には到達できない。技の修練のみにとどまるならば、修行のもたらす最も貴重なものを失うことになる。
我々は真なるものの手前で立ち止まることなく、絶えず真剣に修行を続けなければならないのである。そうすれば、道は開ける。
成功とは、真なるものを目指しての修行に打ち込む人生を生きる中で、おのずと得られるものなのである。

Jeffery M. Brooks, Director
Northampton Karate dojo
ジェフェリー・M・ブルークス
ノーザンプトン空手道場長

1995年12月　同志会

True Karate Dō

GIVING. Giving means having an attitude of generosity toward others, not withholding anything from them: not our knowledge, not our energy, not our kindness. A generous person is someone who generates energy, not someone who looks outward to others to provide it.

MORALITY. The word "morality" may seem to have an antique ring; it may sound like something repressive and restrictive. In our practice it is liberating. By morality we mean not exploiting others, not taking advantage of them for money, power, sex, fame and so on. By respecting others, we create good conditions for practice, freeing ourselves and others from the distraction of disturbance and contention.

PATIENCE. This means patience in the active sense – the resilience required to continue to practice despite the obstacles we encounter. It is the willingness to persevere, to rededicate ourselves day to day, moment to moment, to practice. Patience means persisting without getting angry.

EFFORT. Being nice is not enough. Neither is being tough or talented or tricky. We have received a precious human life – a body, a mind, our talents. We can use them to benefit ourselves and others only if we do not neglect them, only if we make the most of them. Relentless effort is required to avoid becoming distracted by trivialities, to avoid the fickleness, complacency, egotism and rigidity which can thwart the fruitful practice of our art.

MEDITATION. This does not only mean seated meditation. It is a recognition of the need for mindfulness in all the things we do, think and say. It is the practice of stability of mind, leading to concentration, a requisite for profound practice.

The sixth element is WISDOM. To dedicate one's self to a practice aimed at perfection is an all-encompassing undertaking. This is the kind of life we can cultivate through karate. It offers us a way to live fully human lives. By consistently aiming at technical mastery, we move deeper and deeper. Our karate practice must be vigorous, practical and effective. But to stop there is to miss what is most valuable in our practice. Stopping there the real treasure of a karate life remains only a potentiality.

None of us need to stop short of the ultimate. We should just continue to train sincerely, every day. Success not measured externally, but achieved living a life dedicated to the practice of perfection.

-Jeffrey Brooks

Reading this again after all these years it is evident to me that this view set the course for all the work I have done in and out of the dojo, and which I can now relate.

***

Sakiyama's Final Challenge

It was unlikely we would ever meet again. But training was not over. To continue, Sakiyama Roshi, abbot of Kozen-ji Zendo in Shuri, Okinawa, presented me with this:

He asked that I study it; penetrate its truth completely. He urged me to visit his dharma brother when I returned to the US, train with him face-to-face, and see our project through to the end.

Sakiyama's note said:

億劫相別而須臾不離　盡日相対而刹那不対

"Even if one feels they are separated for a time that feels infinite, the truth is they are not separated even by the tiniest amount"

"Furthermore, even if one says they are facing each other all day, the truth is that they are not facing each other at all."

There are several sources for these lines from the early years after Zen was imported to Japan from China, long ago. But there are thousands of lines, from centuries of training, face to face, teacher to student, generation after generation, filling many volumes. From the mountains of books and rivers of talk pouring forth from the tradition beyond words Sakiyama chose those two lines.

The lines are touching. Separation from people in our lives makes us unhappy. Attachment causes trouble. Separation is inevitable. What do we do with it?

The mixture of emotion and idea, formulated for illumination and ignition in the laser light of samadhi, had my attention. No doubt it was a message to his dharma brother, as well as an instruction for me.

The two of them, years before, as young men, sat face to face all night long, practicing in the great temple where they trained. How clear and present the memory was to him, the memory of the two of them, as novices, enchanted by enthusiasm, pouring their hearts into practice, encouraging each other, challenging each other, their aspirations spreading before them, vast as the moonlight. His nostalgia was poignant: the passing away of lifetimes, the old world vanished, naïve hope solidified in the shape of a life already lived. Did he hope I would be the bridge that would connect them once again?

When I met his dharma brother later that year, I showed him a photo of Sakiyama Roshi, which I had taken before I left Okinawa. He held the snapshot, looked at it with curious, warm attention. As he gazed at it, surprise flickered across his princely face. "He got old!" he said.

I had not gotten old. I did not yet know the experience of seeing an old friend after a long separation, and in the changed but familiar face, seeing the passing of time mixed with the vivid pleasure of recollections of things past.

The lines Sakiyama wrote were deeply moving to me. I was young, meeting an old, respected teacher. His presence was imposing. His karate once was powerful. He was a direct student of Miyagi Chojun. His Zen students included Nagamine Shoshin, founder of Matsubayashi Ryu, who introduced me to Zen and to Sakiyama Roshi.

In the lines he gave me to study, Sakiyama's warm-heartedness was evident in a way it rarely was in person.

He asked me to investigate these ideas because, he was telling me, they are true:

"Even if one feels they are separated for a time that feels infinite, the truth is they are not separated even by the tiniest amount"

"Furthermore, even if one says they are facing each other all day, the truth is that they are not facing each other at all."

Examining this statement, gaining insight into it, penetrating it thoroughly, becoming accustomed to a new way of seeing, is how we can use lines like these. Not by intoning the words as if they possessed some magic power of their own. Not by repeating them until their sound dissolves into gibberish. Not by defaulting to perplexity, jangled or placid, using paradox to subvert your rational mind. Not by rejecting discursive thought, or abandoning language.

I was to use these lines as a tool to understand their proposition, and through this understanding, the nature of my own heart and mind.

These two lines express two plain ideas. One is the non-separation of subject-object-action. The other is the no-self nature of persons.

Both ideas are predicated on the seamless, undivided nature of reality. Both are accessible to reason, and to direct experience. Understanding them is the gate to freedom.

A thumbnail of no-self nature of persons: We are made of parts. There is no person within the person. No part is the person by itself. Even the aggregate of the parts is not the person. We change. We are real. We act. We are subject to conditions. We create conditions. Our lives matter. They are of infinite consequence. They extend in time and space. There is nothing esoteric or mysterious in these ideas.

Although it is different from the way we customarily think about ourselves, it is accurate and supported by reason. It does not take years of meditation, an altered state, or genius to understand it. We can all make good use of this.

Understanding it establishes the imperative for moral and ethical conduct, the rationale for developing a calm, clear mind, and the necessity of penetrating the truth. These three together yield freedom from alienation, confusion, conflict and suffering. Insight begins and ends with understanding no-self nature. That is what Sakiyama's "koan" was pointing to. That is why it was so moving and so important that he chose this as his way of saying goodbye.

This rational explanation is no spoiler if you want to use these two lines for your own kensho, because knowing about this and thoroughly penetrating it are different. But you've got to start somewhere.

So, what to do?

This job probably won't get done in an hour a day, like homework or a hobby. It's more like D-Day, except it may last for a lifetime, and you don't know how it will turn out.

The accumulation of insight, pressure, refinement and focus, drilling deeper and deeper consciously and unconsciously, devoting your intelligence, humanity, will and power, continually, and then settling down and letting the words of the koan operate in your heart and mind without manipulation, leads across the phase boundary to insight.

Then, like ice becoming water, or water transformed into vapor, new properties emerge in your experience. The body and mind you always had, the world you always lived in, the words of the instruction themselves have new life and new meaning which were untapped, unusable, and invisible before. They were raw materials. Something happened to change them.

When the 15th century Tibetan master Tsong-khapa achieved his enlightenment, he said it was completely different from what he expected.

If anyone would know what to expect you would think it would be him. You would think. He was a genius. But he didn't. He expected to get out of the mass of suffering. But it turned out he did not "get out." He got in, becoming completely enmeshed in the infinity of living beings.

He said:

··· Train in the spirit of enlightenment which is rooted in love and compassion, and strive to develop this as much as you can. Without it, the practices of the six perfections and the two stages are like stories built on a house with no foundation. ···

Tsong-Kha-Pa. *The Great Treatise On The Stages Of The Path To Enlightenment* Vol 3, p 362

The main flaw in the Zen I met was the premise that cultivating a special condition, a special state of mind via meditation, is the key to freedom.

This is the assumption on which Zen-influenced martial arts base their soteriology. The assumption that perfection will come if you persist – in sitting, in training, in something – is not supported. People who take this on faith are disappointed. Persistence is not enough. Saying "There *is* no goal!" is not an adequate instruction. Saying "Just sit!" misleads untrained people.

I visited Sakiyama's dharma brother several times. It was not what I expected.

Sakiyama's presence was austere and strong. A real karate man. Old as he was, there was no question in his manner; there was certainty in his gaze, purpose in his voice. His temple, called Kozen-ji, was an island of silence and order, a world apart from the traffic-clogged streets and busy shops in the bustling Naha neighborhood.

Eido Roshi, Sakiyama's dharma brother, made a different impression. Not that I am the best judge of character, but he was charming and warm. He welcomed me when I visited. As we talked, he made us bowls of powdered green tea, which he whisked with grace and drank, slurping with relish and elegance, turning his bowl a little each time he took a sip. As we chatted, he waved his hand toward the throng of people out in the hall, sitting in the break room, standing on the veranda. He smiled a little ruefully and said "The roof needs repair. It is very expensive."

He did not explain that. He did not need to. His temple was large, set on 1,400 acres of gently rolling countryside. Herds of deer, heads down, munching, don't even look up as visitors drive by on their way to the temple. They have grass to eat. We have people to see.

Dai Bosatsu, as the temple is called, was designed by Japanese architects and built by Japanese craftsmen, in classic style, with traditional techniques, in the 1970's.

The artisans were brought in to do the work, and paid with a large private donation. Eido Roshi was installed as abbot. He soon found that American Zen culture was not like Zen culture in Japan. In Japan the cultural heft of the tradition put many people off. To them it was a relic, tired, past its time. But others were ardent, profoundly devoted, and when they were in training, were held to high standards.

In America, from the time the Zen Studies Society was formed to assist D.T. Suzuki introduce Zen to the west, Zen attracted some serious people but many others. Beatniks, hippies, and counter-cultural intellectuals who were seeking an alternative to what was for them bland, conformist, materialist, uptight, repressed post-war American culture.

They found the discipline of Zen appealing, at least in theory. They found the aesthetic, with its visual simplicity infused with obvious opulence, reassuring. The people Eido Roshi waved his hand toward on the day of my first visit, were new.

Maybe they were just dabbling. Trying out a weekend retreat to see if they would get anything out of it. They were not familiar with the mores or the purpose of the place they were visiting. No one seemed to know how to brief them.

One woman, smiling, delighted, came a few steps into the office where we were talking and said "Good dharma, Roshi!"

Eido smiled at her and nodded, and glanced at me as if to say "This is what I put up with to raise the money to fix the roof."

I did not know exactly what she meant. He did not seem to know either. She was trying to be nice, but was not familiar with the jargon or the customs. He seemed to take it for granted that visitors would be clueless.

 My impression was that Eido did not know what to do with these visitors, what to do with his place in the world, or what to make of it all.

He did not know how to turn untutored worldlings into dharma practitioners. He did not know where to start. I am not sure if he was interested. He knew this was not the way it worked back home.

He was removed from his position as abbot after numerous complaints about his behavior with females. He died a few years later.

In Japan the job of a Zen priest is, in a way, a job. Priests lead rituals, operate the temple, lead meditation, and sometimes practice too, but that is not required. There, since priests are mainly married and have children, their lives are as embedded in the life of the community as anyone else's. They are not monks, living at a distance, modeling an ideal of life beyond the concerns of this world.

In America the visitors were not seeking a ceremonial officiant, they were interested in liberation, as mentioned frequently in Zen talks, books and art. These visitors had heard a lot about liberation in college.

It was a good thing. Or maybe it was many good things. Liberation was international politics, as in revolutionary movements around the world. Liberation was sexual politics, as in overthrowing the patriarchy. Liberation was engaging in sexual activity without the artificial constraints of fidelity, responsibility, consequences, warmth or children.

There was so much churn around this particular kind of liberation that the line between sex and power moved so frequently it began to wear thin, where there was a line. So, without the constraints of community and cultural tradition, believe it or not some of these American Zen groups took on the shape not of an exalted human enterprise but of an ordinary primate band. With a big fellow at the top, and the other members of the band competing for favors, attention and ascent in the hierarchy.

Zen, in those days, did not teach the healthy personal behavior known as moral and ethical conduct. Although some groups did pick up that thread after generations of difficulties.

But even at first, people did know or should have known that promiscuity leads inevitably to loneliness and anger. This was not news anywhere in the world. Buddhism teaches this explicitly. Zen, at least in those days, did not.

This dominance dynamic operates in every group to some degree. It is not just chimps that use it. Every corporation, mafia, sports team, university faculty, political organization, martial arts group, religious organization or police department that I have been around has. Where there are objective measures of performance, and competence is valued, then people develop discipline and self-restraint. With good leadership, ascent in the hierarchy is based on merit and is recognized by the members as justified.

But without a way to measure competence, without specific requirements for performance, with attendant incentives and penalties, then friction, disappointment and dispute are inevitable.

I do not know if Eido went off the rails and became a predator, and that he took many unwanted actions toward vulnerable females. But this is what they said he did. He has been cancelled and his name has disappeared from the temple website. I imagine the chance to get Zen started in America seemed like a great opportunity at first. I imagine, by the end, he wished he stayed home.

The warning appears in the oldest sources, including the Samyutta Nikaya, from thousands of years ago:

> **Gain, honor and praise are dreadful.**
> **An obstacle for beginners who attract devotion,**
> **And for accomplished practitioners···**

After 2,500 years the advice is still fresh. It applies to all of us. When novices enter a religious life, people think they are holy, even though they really are just beginners, learning their way, easily tempted, distracted and confused.

When experienced people achieve prominence, they are subject to flattery. It is pleasant. It feels deserved. They too can lose their way. It is a long road back to the austere iconoclasm of mountain Ch'an. It is a long road to any genuine religious life. And there are only a few signs pointing the way.

It may be that there was no golden age to return to. It may be that there were people, great and small, trying to find their way. Whatever there was, the Ch'an school in China undermined its practice imperative with theory, long ago. The effect persists. The doctrinal claim that we are all already Buddhas took the fire out of practice. That this might have been understood as completion stage tantra seemed not to come up. People were unprepared. It led to confusion.

(The philosophical subversion of technical knowledge and practical experience is explained by Carl Bielefeldt in *Dogen's Manuals of Zen Meditation*.)

The cult of the Zen master as the sole source of wisdom and authority, the exclusive claim of "mind-to-mind" transmission within the tradition, the rejection of ideas and inference, exaggerated it. Eager neophytes in our time, educated in post-modern anti-language and habituated in self-regard, may have failed to grasp the non-grasping mind.

億劫相別而須臾不離 盡日相対而刹那不対

"Even if one feels they are separated for a time that feels infinite, the truth is they are not separated even by the tiniest amount"

Is this pointing to the Dharmakaya, the truth body, one nature, no separation in time, space or mind, to no one to be separated?

"Furthermore, even if one says they are facing each other all day, the truth is that they are not facing each other at all."

Does this point to the no self-nature of persons? Although we are people, real and alive, the boundaries and character which we assume define us are more fluid, subtle and magnificent than what we, by habit, see.

*

I asked Eido Roshi about the relationship between martial arts and liberation. I asked him if he thought that religious practice and martial practice could really lead to the same place. He did not answer immediately. We practiced together, we talked for a while. Then he took out his brush and two shodo cards and he brushed his answer to me. My understanding of his answer has completely changed.

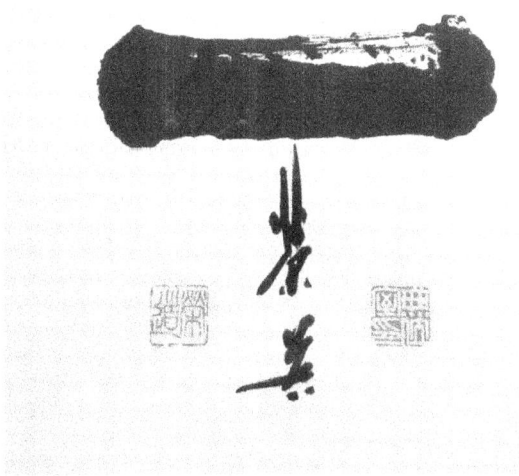

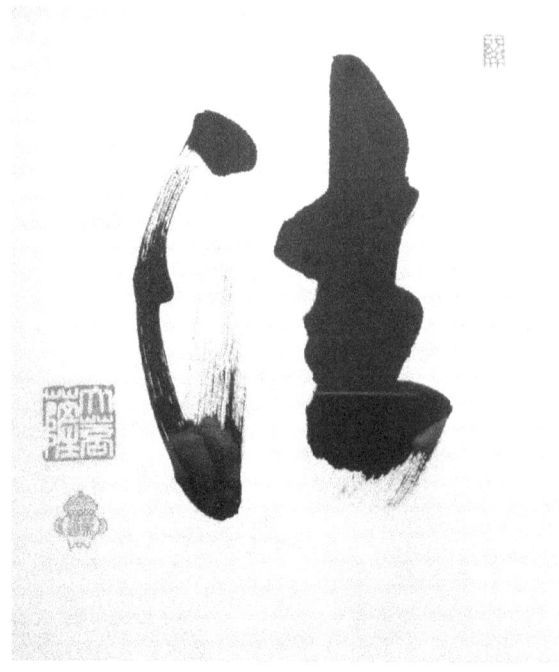

The point here is not to judge practitioners, past or present. I do not know their minds. The literature they left us is not always illuminating. But we have to make judgements and choices for ourselves, choices of what to pick up and what to set aside.

The proposition in Zen-influenced martial arts is that you can reach ultimate human perfection by cultivating a clear mind, or a still mind, or a content-free mind. It seemed to me that, distracted by an idea they did not understand, like devotees of a cargo cult waiting for their ship to come in, practitioners overlooked the rewards of transformation which really are available.

Profound transformation comes when you understand that your conduct, your ethics, your moral commitments, your personal responsibility for the well-being of others, and the cultivation of a generous heart is indispensable for reaching the goal. Then you will be moved to push beyond your limits, mastering your body, mind and skill, to devote all to the people who need you.

There is no separation between us and what we have done. There will be no distance between what we do and what we will face.

This is not easy to find in Sakiyama's farewell koan. But it is there.

***

NOTES:

> Thanks to Jeremy Blaustein for translation assistance.

- The source of the quotation Sakiyama chose is linked to Kamakura era priest Shuho Myocho, later Daito Kokushi 大燈国師. Japan's National History University Encyclopedia cites him:

"They've been separated for a long time, for eternity, but haven't been separated even for a short time. Moreover, they are facing each other all day long, but they are not facing each other."

- The four dhyanas of the Buddhist eight-fold path's "right concentration" are not the same as mushin or "no-mind." Sources vary in interpretation of the dhyanas but they are characterized by single-pointed absorption in an object of meditation, attending to objects of increasing subtlety, and conditions of mind of increasing tranquility. They establish the basis for insight meditation, the next step on the gradual path to enlightenment in the early Buddhist traditions. The dhyanas are also the condition of mind to which the Arhats, people who completed the path, return, as a "pleasant abiding" in this life.

Mushin, No-mind as described in the Japanese budo traditions, does not correspond to this meditative experience, in its technique, content or purpose. While the subjective experience of the engagement of the will and cognition vanish to the conscious mind of the Zen budo practitioner, according to the lore, the practitioner remains engaged in purpose and action, even in the experience of mushin – sweeping the temple courtyard, or fighting with swords, for example.

Since the Japanese name "Zen" derives from the Chinese "Ch'an", which is a pronunciation of the Pali word "jhana" or the Sanskrit word "dhyana", this labeling has caused some confusion, since the same words mean different things.

- The position that 8th Century Chinese Ch'an priest "Ha-Shang Mahayana" took on 'no-thought' is addressed in Tsong Khapa's *Lam Rim Chen Mo*, vol 2, p87. This reference notes the omission of the cultivation of bodhicitta and the six perfections in Ch'an. This omission is reflected in the Zen budo of Musashi, Takuan and others. This fact does not diminish their budo. It addresses the claim of ultimate liberation and fulfillment of human potential through their budo. The words emptiness, liberation, nirvana and others are the same across these traditions but they seem to mean different things.

- The "content-less mind" of "Ha-Shang Mahayana," who propounded the Ch'an view, may not be an emptiness meditation at all. **"(Jigme Lingpa) argues that, if the meditator attempts to stop conceptual activity without distinguishing between mind *(sems)* and awareness (*rig pa)*, the result is a blank indeterminacy (*lung ma bstan*). In awareness, he argues, conceptualization is neutralized in a state that is "like a crystal ball", a simile which points to clarity and vividness, rather than indeterminacy and blankness. –** Sam van Schaik

- For the Mahayana view of no-self nature of persons: p289, vol. III <u>Lam Rim Chen Mo</u>; for the Theravada view: <u>Selfless Persons</u>, by Steven Collins

***

What Sakiyama Saw

After sharing some of Sakiyama's comments with friends, training partners and others, after discussing his encouraging response to my vision for karate practice, I heard from a number of people who made it clear how much Sakiyama Roshi's words echoed in their hearts. His words about karate, his commitment and seriousness, inspired them.

But some people said that in his words to me, in his translation of my writing, and what he said about it, that they could tell he saw something extraordinary in me. I do not think this is the right conclusion to draw.

I am not sure that what he saw. But since we all study and we all teach (whether we know it or not) it is worth considering what he saw, as it may be relevant to our practice relationships.

I believe what he saw was that I was listening. I valued his experience and his advice. I intended to put it into practice. I do not think it is possible to infer anything more than that from what he said and did.

But that is more than enough to make an exchange valuable, to both teacher and student.

When we parted company for the last time, it was because he was persuaded that an active engagement with the six perfections was an interpolation that had no place in Zen. Maybe he was right, viewed from within the conventions of his doctrinal and practice tradition. But I was sure they were indispensable components of a life well-lived, including any life directed to realization, liberation and to the fulfillment of the vows we took when we entered the path. And essential to a healthy dojo.

I listened carefully to what he said, and I learned from him.

***

Part Two
Approach to Kensho

Introduction

In **Damatte Keiko** I introduced the metaphor of a thermodynamic phase transformation – ice to water to steam – to describe karate training as more than an accumulation of skills but instead, as a process of the gradual transformation in the heat and pressure of consistent training. The result is a "phase transformation" in which new properties emerge in the practitioner.

In the next section, **Mushin and the Science of Flow**, I will describe the emergent properties of the skilled and well-conditioned practitioner. I will show that the condition of body and mind described in the current scientific research on high performance – in athletics, music, and many other fields – maps onto the descriptions of high-performance states in the Japanese Zen-influenced martial arts of the samurai period.

This phase is characterized by intense concentration, clear goals, continual feedback on the quality of your performance, and a good match between the level of challenge and the practitioner's level of skill. We use these continually in martial arts training to produce a deep flow state. By using them we go beyond them.

From there I will examine claims of experiences beyond the flow state, - kensho, insight, satori, liberation, Buddhahood, awakening and enlightenment – which are said to be accessible to virtuoso practitioners of the martial arts. These claims are frequently encountered in the literature of Japanese budo, old and new, and have been applied to Okinawan karate, by Sakiyama Roshi and many others. They posit a transition, beyond flow, to a completely realized human life.

The phase transition from the second to the third phase – from mushin (flow) to kensho (seeing) – is approached gradually and crossed suddenly – like the thermodynamic phase transformations in which water changes state, from solid to liquid and liquid to vapor, as heat is added.

In the case of martial arts, the "material" which transforms is us.

Assessing the validity of these claims is a practical matter. One of the reasons people continue to train for a lifetime is the sense that every hour of practice, every kata, every move, every breath is taking them toward their final, ultimate destination.

Their progress, as they practice on this path, combines the worldly benefits of training – strength, speed, skill, determination, agility, confidence, awareness, calm and self-defense – with a transcendent purpose which gives form to life, extending the meaning of practice beyond conventional, world-bound limits. As practitioners get older, while their skills are high and their athleticism is declining, a new aspiration, beyond physical achievement, beyond worldly purpose, is necessary. If the claims of budo as a path to liberation are valid, there is continuing purpose and urgency. If not, practitioners need to know that. And they need to find a way forward.

The people I cite below are influential in Japanese martial arts culture. To make the most of the investigation of these issues, and to put the resulting insights to work, it will be useful to see how the tradition formulates its path and goals.

Mushin and the Science of Flow

Moonlight sent long blue shadows across the snow. There were no streetlights. Just stars. There were about thirty of us there. Whatever hesitation or second thoughts there may have been, as people left their families, their homes, their warm cars, to meet at this spot at this hour, were over.

We better get moving. It's too cold to stand still. Anyway, there's nothing more to say. We all knew what to do. We began.

The outdoor training that day lasted about 10 hours. As we finished our workout the sun was setting behind the trees. The shadows of the treetops were at our feet.

We came inside, all thirty of us, to stretch in the warmth of the dojo. We knelt on the hard wood floor. Kneeling on the polished wood felt luxurious – so comfortable after hours of training in the cold, on the sloping ground, on uneven ice and snow, in the wind. Deep silence descends as we sit. Steam rises from our bodies, from the top of our heads, from our sweat-soaked uniforms. Everyone feels deep peace. Purified in the heat and pressure of training. There was nothing left to be done.

We were there because it was where we wanted to be. We were not just taking on a challenge. We were rewarded with a deep experience we all knew well.

Phase Transformation through Karate

This phase transition is sometimes described as entering a state of "flow" or "the zone." The Japanese budo terms renzoku, zanshin, mushin, immoveable mind, unstoppable mind, unfettered mind and others point to aspects of this experience.

Central to Human Life for a Million Years

For most of human history optimizing the performance of the body and mind, often in a group setting, was a fundamental necessity for human life. It was the key to our survival in a capricious and hostile world. Self-mastery was an object of passionate interest, and a central focus of traditional research and development, east and west.

That changed.

In the last few centuries, as the crisis of the wars of religion spawned the philosophical enlightenment, as the scientific revolution, the industrial revolution, the information age, have given way to the age of automata, the collective human enterprise, east and west, has sought refuge in the world of material, demoting inner exploration to the periphery.

It's back

In some quarters inner exploration is returning to the center of human concern, this time through scientific research. Insights drawn from new research in psychology and neuroscience are governing innovation in communication, politics, athletics, music, gaming, business, the military, law enforcement, education, the arts, engineering and technology, and other areas.

What scientists have found, measured and named, as they investigated the characteristics of human high-performance, matches discoveries made by great masters of Japanese budo centuries ago.

The discoveries in the field of human high-performance have been news to science. The ideas are not news to practitioners of traditional arts, but the science is useful to us because the language is accessible, the analysis is careful, and the research recommends specific steps we can take to more efficiently master our martial arts.

For example, research shows that there is a set of qualities shared by high-performers in all fields. These include: Intense concentration. Focus on action in the present moment. Continuous vitality and fluidity. Confidence in your own ability. And certainty that your actions will get results.

When we acquire those qualities, through training, we pass a "phase boundary." This is not only the result of a quantitative increase in skill from practice. There is a qualitative change too: new "emergent properties" arise in our body and mind, as a result of our training.

We can feel it. Our subjective experience tells us when we have passed the phase boundary, and entered a "flow" state.

These subjective impressions are familiar to long-term practitioners of combatives: We experience time differently – long periods seem to pass in an instant, and rapid-fire encounters seem to unfold in slow motion; we are freed from a preoccupation with ourselves, our mundane concerns and anything outside our immediate field of action. As we cross the boundary to the flow phase, we feel that what we are doing is worth doing for its own sake. We are not seeking an extrinsic reward. We do not want or need one.

This is why my group gathered outside the dojo on that cold winter morning, in the ice and snow, for a long outdoor workout in the moonlight. That is why I scheduled it. That is what we got from doing it.

Japanese Zen master Takuan Soho, advised his client, sword master Yagyu Munenori:

"No-mind is the same as right mind. It neither hardens nor remains static. It is called no-mind when the mind has neither discrimination nor a single thought, but moves unimpeded through the whole body and extends through the entire self.

"The no-mind is placed nowhere. Yet it is not like wood or stone.

"When this no-mind has been well-developed the mind does not come to rest on one thing nor does it miss anything…."

"No mind" has been sometimes misinterpreted as an instruction to "blank out your mind." That is not what Takuan taught. His advice was practical. It was a corrective to mental rigidity and the tactical formulae that obstruct high performance. He is describing a flow state.

Musashi Miyamoto, in "Emptiness," the final chapter of his Book of Five Rings, highlights the importance of "Mushin," No-Mind – a flow state, in which an experienced martial practitioner has sufficient skill to respond spontaneously to the changing dynamics of a combative encounter, and turn them to advantage, without consciously thinking. Musashi also uses the word Munen, No-thought, to describe this same flow state of spontaneous skillful action. There is no correspondence between what Musashi is describing and Buddhist "enlightenment" understood either as insight into dependent origination and impermanence, direct perception of the four noble truths, or as direct perception of emptiness. There is correspondence between his description and a high flow state.

In his 18th century allegory of the art of the sword called "Nekko no Myojutsu" or "The Cat's Subtle Art", Issai Chozan describes the limitations of technique, of spirit, of cunning and of intention, and he charts a developmental path to mastery – ascent through flow states which arise through martial training.

He advises, as a means to overcome the limitations of the conventional training techniques of martial prowess, the cultivation of Mushin – which he presents as "no thought, no mind and no conscious effort of will."

He is describing the entry into a state of flow.

Mushin, "No-mind", Issai says, allows the fighter to pierce the veil of self-centered dualism, which he identifies as the key impediment to freedom of action. This clarity leads to victory.

Some understand the cultivation of "no-mind" as a recommendation to adopt a particular mind-state. It does not, because that does not work. What this material does advocate is relentless practice, which yields deep transformation: harmonizing and uniting body and mind, dropping off conscious effort of will, thought, or planning, as the mind and body of the practitioner become pliant, skillful and spontaneous in action.

This is what it means to pass the phase transition boundary.

Knowing the words of these masters helps us. It gives us the tools to recognize the state we are entering as our training is underway, so that we can cultivate it efficiently.

Another term used in Japanese budo which describes a characteristic of the flow state is "Zanshin." This describes "continuing awareness", literally "continuing mind." Present without being stuck, open without being vague, aware of what is present without embellishment, able to sense the emerging possibilities in each changing moment.

It is an urgent, practical matter for a fighter to use this. It is not esoteric, intellectual, or remote. High-performers use it, whether they label it or not. It is accessible. It is experienced in the flow phase of human performance.

In kumite, fighting, if your mind is distracted or spaced out, even for a split second, when you are facing an alert opponent, you will get immediate and unpleasant feedback. You learn from it – that feedback is an essential component of entering flow. If your opponent looks down, or darts his eyes over your shoulder, you will detect it instantly and if you can, exploit the suki, the gap in his defense. If you succeed, he will try hard not to let it happen again. Improvement comes for both fighters. Both go deeper into flow by means of the cycle of error, immediate feedback, and re-engagement in ongoing practice, with no deflection of mental focus.

When we are able to sustain our attention, without interruption or fluctuation, that is zanshin, continuing mind.

Flow and Group Flow

Starting in the 1970s psychologist Mihaly Csíkszentmihályi wrote about his research into high-performance states of mind, which he called "Flow."

Relevant to traditional karate dojo practice, researchers have identified a phenomenon they call "group flow." We know it well. When members of a team, band, military unit, business or dojo cooperate, agree on goals, skills and patterns of action, then "social flow," or group cohesion, emerges.

Team challenges stimulate the group to cohere more completely and enter a flow state as a group. Through group training the group progresses toward maximum performance.

Also relevant to dojo practice: group flow positively correlates with higher commitment to the group and higher motivation to personal mastery. This is good for the group and for every member in it.

Observing Flow in Others

You can observe "flow" in other people and you can hear it too: in a band that's tight, a military unit that's high-speed, low-drag, a great athlete who is in the zone, a great team where every player knows what they need to do, and anticipates what everyone else will do.

Experience and Measurement of Flow

Individuals in a flow state all report being totally absorbed in what they were doing; they felt elevated; they knew what they needed to do and they knew they had the skills to do it. They expressed a sense of timelessness – focused on the present while time passed quickly. And they found that in flow the experience itself was its own reward.

Physiological measurements confirm what practitioners experience. As a performer enters a flow state, their heart rate and blood pressure decrease and the facial muscles relax. Flow is known in the old literature, in the new research, and in the hearts and minds of practitioners everywhere, as a state of effortless attention. It will not surprise accomplished climbers, rowers, runners, pilots, medics, team athletes, musicians, or martial artists, that the effortless attention and overall relaxation of the body and mind does not impede performance; it enhances it.

Mimetic Praxis: Flow is Hijacked by Entertainment and Remote Managers

Although performers enter a flow state when they perform, the people watching them – observers, managers, coaches, audiences and fans – do not. Entertainment hijacks "flow." Watching images and sounds does not engage the same suite of mental functions as self-directed, purposeful attention which engages your will, analytical and planning functions in goal-oriented action – the conditions which produce a flow state.

This hijacking of the perceptual and emotional apparatus of flow, without developing it through skills and challenges, is why entertainment can become intoxicating and in the long run, debilitating.

The distinction between flow and entertainment is obvious: audience members are not engaged in action – they do not have personal control, agency, or a performance-feedback loop – all essential for mastery and flow.

From the perspective of neuroscience – audience members lack what participants get from training: the harmony of brain wave patterns, the training of the will and cognition and affect, and the union of psychological and somatic action. These happen in a flow state. They do not happen when you watch someone else perform.

Kata, Kumite and Flow

In kumite we concentrate intensely and we get immediate feedback on the quality of our performance. In matches where the skill level of the opponents is close, and the rules and objectives are clear, we can train in flow states. By using kata to deepen our skills, and increasing the level of challenge incrementally over time, with consistent feedback from instructors, we can produce high skills and readily make the phase transition to a flow state.

Training the Hara

The modern science of flow confirms another central premise of traditional training: Karate practice has been described as "training the hara."

In one sense the hara refers to the center of the body, the center of gravity, the center of energy. But in pre-modern Japanese and Okinawan cultures the hara referred to the seat of the will. Training the hara in karate meant making your will powerful. How important is that to high-performance in combatives and other demanding high-skill activities? It is not just a tool in the toolkit. It is central.

Getting the moves "right" will not win a fight. Filling the form of the techniques with "spirit" by taking the initiative, dominating the opponent and leading the dynamics of the engagement, are essential. That is a function of a strong will – used with good judgment, accessible by choice, where and when it may be needed.

Research shows that goal-directed behavior – willed action – reduces our susceptibility to distractions – which consume our limited attentional resources. It does this by chemically suppressing the stimulus-response systems of the brain.

This is supported by the subjective experience reported by high-performers. Bill Lewinski, director of the Force Science Institute:

···It is characteristic of great athletic performance where athletes—operating in complex and dynamic situations under high levels of physiological and emotional arousal—utilize focus, experience, and training for great decision making and performance. It's not surprising that many of the law enforcement and military personnel I have interviewed have credited their survival and ability to save others on their decision to focus on what needed to be done in the moment, despite the life-threatening and chaotic circumstances they were operating in."

In other words, intention overcomes distraction. That is both an attitude and a mental function which we train in the flow phase in karate.

Implications for Dojo Classes

Researcher Steven Kotler writing in the *Harvard Business Review*, listed four conditions that produce a flow state – intense concentration, goal clarity, feedback as to how well you are doing, and a properly matched challenge to skills ratio. We use these continually in martial arts training.

If the challenge level is set lower than the skill level of the practitioner, they will not enter a flow state, will not improve, will not enjoy class and will get bored. Some instructors try to remedy boredom in their students by adding more curriculum – more katas, more weapons, more talk about "the old way", more ranks, patches and other extrinsic rewards. That does not work.

What does work, according to the science of flow and practical dojo experience, is making sure that the level of challenge in the class matches the level of skill of the students. That will keep classes exciting. This is why 'repetition' of kata is not useful, but doing kata many times while focusing on investigating different aspects of them, with varied intensity, and the presentation of body mechanics, energy flows, interpretation and applications, does.

If the challenge level is set much higher than the practitioner's skill level then the practitioner will feel anxiety and eventually failure. They will not cross the phase boundary and will not enter a flow state.

Modulating the challenge-to-skill ratio during the course of a class produces a phase of high-challenge within tolerable and helpful levels of stress, followed by a phase of moderate-challenge, which promotes confidence-building and recovery.

Using multiple, well-calibrated cycles of this kind in each class is an effective way to maximize technical competence and conditioning and producing phase transition to flow. This is true in all disciplines. We can use these insights in the dojo.

Department of Defense Flow Research

DARPA, the Defense Advanced Research Projects Agency, one of the world's most famous top-secret military research institutions, investigated the effects of flow on human performance. They found that inducing flow states in military snipers during training cut their training-time-to-proficiency in half. Following training the induced flow state multiplied the shooter's performance measures by a factor of five.

That impressive result confirms what martial arts theorists and practitioners have been advocating for at least 500 years.

Happiness

Habituating to operating in a flow state requires: clear goals, high challenge, performance feedback, completely engagement in purposeful action, being in control, feeling that your efforts matter. As you pass the phase boundary to flow, you experience a merging of action and awareness. Your action becomes spontaneous and effective.

These conditions are associated with high performance and, researchers have observed, are strongly correlated to happiness. People who are accustomed to flow appear happy, self-confident and relaxed.

It is also why flow-inducing activity is appealing: it makes you feel good.

Variations in Flow

You do not have to be a professional performer or competitor to enter a flow state. You do not have to be a karate or sword master to enter Mushin. There are as many variations of flow as there are people.

Using the analogy of phase changes of H_2O – as ice passes the phase boundary, melts, and becomes water: no one thinks that water has only one way of being water. It can be cool, warm or hot; it can be moving or still, turbulent or smooth, cloudy or clear, and on and on with infinite variations. Despite the variations it remains water in the liquid phase.

It is the same way with practitioners. Flow is not one thing. Within the category of flow or Mushin are variations, with some consistent characteristics that define the state.

It is possible for us to make our flow state deep, clear, strong and reliable as we train. So, if you can get a few dozen people who have been training together for years to meet out under the stars for a long day of training, the experience can be spectacular.

*

Notes:

1. Sports Psychology Today http://www.sportpsychologytoday.com/youth-sports-psychology/understanding-the-zone-in-sports/

2. Nature Neuroscience Yoshida, K., Drew, M.R., Mimura, M. et al. Serotonin-mediated inhibition of ventral hippocampus is required for sustained goal-directed

behavior. Nat Neurosci 22, 770– 777 (2019) doi:10.1038/s41593-019-0376-5 [ ]

3. Force Science Institute https://www.forcescience.org/2019/12/when-theres-no-time-to-breathe-expert-focus-for-elite-performance/

4. Harvard Business Review https://hbr.org/2014/05/create-a-work-environment-that-fosters-flow

5. Positive Psychology https://positivepsychology.com/what-is-flow/

6. Podium Sports Journal https://www.podiumsportsjournal.com/2010/10/01/how-to-achieve-the-flow-state-in-athletics-and-life/

7. The Knockout Game, Is "Nothing" Sacred, Zanshin – essays on MountainKarateNC.com

8. The Good Fight – The Virtues and Value of the Martial Arts by Jeffrey M. Brooks

9. The Rhinoceros Tale – Martial Arts and the Path to Freedom by Jeffrey M. Brooks

10. Csíkszentmihályi is usually pronounced "Chick sent me hi".

***

The Zen culture of Zen budo

> "Satori is the raison d'etre of Zen."
> – D.T. Suzuki

D.T. Suzuki, probably the most influential Japanese scholar of the 20th century, led the import of Zen to the west. He was for decades its primary proponent, apologist and scholar. In the quote above he is stating that Satori, complete enlightenment, is what Zen is and what Zen is for. In his books such as <u>Zen in Japanese Culture</u>, and as quoted below, he makes it clear that the purpose and method of Zen extend to the Japanese Zen-influenced martial arts.

I have used the thermodynamic analogy because the way water changes when it freezes or boils is familiar to all of us, eastern or western, practitioner or not.

There are many transformation schemes describing the path of practice from initiation to completion used in

Zen and Japanese Zen-budo to describe and map the path of practice.

Shu Ha Ri

The three stages of training called "Shu Ha Ri", 守破離, first appeared in the 12th century. It was used in traditional Zen aesthetics, beginning with the art of tea, and was adopted by Noh theater, kendo, Japanese sword fighting, and modern martial arts.

The terms "Shu Ha Ri" can be interpreted as 'keeping the form,' 'breaking out of the form,' and 'departing from the form.' This is not esoteric. Long-term training which remains vital and alive, works this way. The meaning of the first two stages – 1. learning and preserving the form through diligent practice, and 2. embodying the form in flow – is clear. The last stage "ri", or hanareru, "to leave behind" or "to become distant," does not describe a particular way of practice or a result of training. It hints.

Budo expert Trevor Leggett observed that this stage is often omitted in modern Japan, where rote repetition is as far as most people go. But it is not only in Japan or in modern times that this is so. Virtuoso practice is rare. It requires patient and persistent effort under continuous challenge for decades.

Deshimaru Taisen

20th Century Zen sword master Taisen Deshimaru, disciple of Soto Zen master Kodo Sawaki, Roshi, describes the stage of the path of practice this way, in his book <u>The Zen Way to the Martial Arts:</u>

···The first (stage) shojin, is the period of training in which the will and the conscious effort are involved, and which generally takes some three to five years of diligent practice··· The second stage is the period of concentration without consciousness··· The disciple is at peace··· In the third stage, the spirit achieves true freedom···

His second stage, the disciple at peace, seems to describe an unperturbable, purposeful flow state. As for his third stage: What characterizes this "true freedom"? It depends on who you read or who you ask. But achieving the ideal of "freedom" is consistently presented as the goal of martial arts training in the Japanese Zen-budo tradition.

The Five Path Sequence of the Heart Sutra

The Heart Sutra is a Buddhist scripture central to many east Asian Buddhist traditions. It is chanted in Zen monasteries several times a day, every day. It is an encapsulation of the metaphysics of Mahayana Buddhism. It maps a path of practice to enlightenment.

It compresses the elaborate doctrinal presentations of long expositions – such as the 8,000-, 25,000- or 100,000-verse Prajna Paramita sutras – into a single page of text. It expresses the ideas at the heart of the Zen understanding of the nature of reality and the way to realize it, and thereby, to be liberated forever from craving and ignorance, realizing the deathless, the unconditioned state of nirvana.

The Heart Sutra informs practice and the practice rationale in the Zen-budo schools.

In the Heart Sutra the constituents of existence are listed and then, in turn, each is negated. The point is that not one of these familiar constituents of existence exists by itself, but exist only as a flow, a process, as a temporary assembly of parts, depending on one another, arising from causes and conditions, all of which are continually changing, becoming other things.

It is sometimes misinterpreted as nihilistic, as a denial of the existence of phenomena. People unfamiliar with the doctrinal view the sutra is presenting may interpret its words as claiming that the things listed do not exist. This is an error. When the sword masters Musashi Miyamoto, Yagyu Munenori and others who I cite later, direct their practice to Satori, or "enlightenment," the language they use and the method they use to approach it, reflect their understanding of the Heart Sutra and similar presentations.

Note: The text of the Heart Sutra and the further notes appear in Appendix One.

At the end of the Heart Sutra, a Mahayana Buddhist sutra, is a single line that suggests a Vajrayana Buddhist esoteric connection. (The historical Shaolin Temple tradition was devoted to Vajrayana tantra. The Japanese Buddhist warrior tradition, associated with Zen, also had a strong esoteric association, as did many Chinese martial traditions during the Ming and Ching eras. The Nio guardian deity at Japan's Kofuku-ji temple, seen on the cover of the English edition of Funakoshi Gichin's <u>Karate Do Kyohan</u>, is from this tradition.)

This connection echoes in the mantra at the end of the Heart Sutra – GA-te, GA-te, PAra-ga-te, PAra-sum-ga-te, BOdhi svA-ha – a succinct formulation of the path to enlightenment. This mantra, retained in Sanskrit, not translated into Japanese like the rest of the sutra, lays out a five-step scheme which is sourced from a key Mahayana commentary, the Abhisamayalamkara. The mantra serves as a panoramic overview that reminds practitioners of what they are up to, every time they chant it.

The Five Paths

In the thermodynamic example, a single material – H_2O – transforms from ice to water to vapor, as the material receives energy in the form of heat. In the Heart Sutra scheme, a novice practitioner at stage one begins the heat and pressure of training. At stage two, he enters the path of preparation as a bodhisattva-in-training – a being devoted to acquiring the virtue and wisdom needed to reach enlightenment, to accumulate the immense skill, wisdom and compassion needed to help all beings. At stage three, as the transformative process continues, this practitioner has a first, brief glimpse of liberation, called kensho. The practitioner continues on through deeper and deeper insight, through stage four, habituation, to stage five, Satori – Buddhahood or final liberation.

These five-step mantra:

GA-te, GA-te, PAra-ga-te, PAra-sum-ga-te, BOdhi svA-ha

This map of the practice path, the presumption of its veracity, and faith in its efficacy, were derived originally from Indian Buddhism. This was transmitted through the Chinese Taoist interpretation of Buddhism, transmitted again to Japan, and via Japanese Zen, to the rest of the world. The mantra is sometimes rendered in English as "Gone, Gone, Gone beyond, Gone completely beyond, Enlightenment!"

It was applied to Japanese Zen-budo from the 13th century on. It was conveyed, explicitly and by cultural convention, through centuries of practice, literature and lore. Its influence was pervasive in the Japanese arts, but is present in Chinese, Okinawan and Korean arts as well.

Initially it corresponds in structure to the steps described in the thermodynamic analogy, in which the beginner undergoes the heat and pressure of training and under the right conditions emerges into a flow state of high performance and exhilaration. This transformation is well documented in modern scientific theory, in observation of the natural world, and in research in human high-performance. It is widely applied in athletics, music, leadership, combatives, and religion.

In light of this, two questions, relevant to all martial artists practicing in east Asian traditions, ought to be answered:

1. Can we realize the transformation into deep Flow or Mushin, by devotion to martial arts practice?

The answer presented in ancient manuscripts, in the Ming and Ching martial arts literature, in the medieval Japanese Zen-budo literature, in books, in movies, and claimed by many confident teachers, is unanimously Yes. This transformation is not automatic. It does not just happen because you train a lot. But it can be achieved.

I have plenty of evidence that it is true and that people do it. The evidence is in the performance and the demeanor of accomplished practitioners. I have experienced this throughout my life of practice. There is no question that the process works, and the achievement of deep flow states is accessible.

But the question remains:

2. Can we reach ultimate liberation through martial arts practice?

Is it possible to achieve true perfection, eternal freedom from suffering, omniscience, the knowledge and ability to save all beings from suffering forever, the unconditioned, the deathless, the consummation of our human potential, to transcend the limits of ordinary experience, in other words to achieve complete liberation, also called nirvana and Satori? Devotees of Japanese Zen-budo consistently make this claim.

I will report on my exploration of that claim in the next section. I do not engage in this exploration as a scholar,

I am not one, or to construct a theory, I don't need one, or even to take a position to advocate or debate. I am seeking the best course of action to realize my aims in practice.

Zen Budo grows from Zen Culture

The following paragraph was written by Japanese scholar D.T. Suzuki. The lines are from his introduction to the English edition of <u>Zen in the Art of Archery</u>, by Eugen Herrigel, written in 1953. Here Suzuki characterizes the ultimate stage of Zen-martial arts:

…When this is attained, man thinks yet he does not think. He thinks like the showers coming down from the sky; he thinks like the waves rolling on the ocean; he thinks like the stars illuminating the nightly heavens; he thinks like the green foliage shooting forth in the relaxing spring breeze. Indeed, he is the showers, the ocean, stars, the foliage…
-Suzuki Daisetsu Teitarō (1870-1966)

This is his poetic description of the ultimate level of achievement in Zen-infused Japanese martial arts. Suzuki says "When this is attained…". We could ask "When what is attained?" Do we assume we know? We could answer "Kensho" or "Satori", but that would leave the question unanswered. All the similes he uses are magnificent, natural, and occur spontaneously.

"What is it?" shodo by Japanese Zen abbot

As a detective I would hear eye witness accounts that at first sounded coherent and credible. But when examined, it would turn out that people were filling in the blanks. They weren't lying. They just figured. When asked about these spots in their story they would say something like: "Well, it must have been..." "How else could it have gotten there?" "I just thought…"

We all fill in the blanks. To make sense of the evidence. To orient in an unfamiliar or changing landscape. To get a good match for what we expect to be true. But that is not adequate. Not if we want to get to the truth.

That is not adequate for a martial artist who wants to master their body, their mind, their art, their attacker. Not for someone pursuing inner training aimed at freedom. It is not adequate if you want to protect people.

Suzuki's claim for the exalted potential of martial arts training is an article of faith in Japanese Zen-budo and in other east Asian martial arts traditions. It has been embraced by many in the West.

If we can confirm it then it will inspire us and guide us. If we cannot then there is more work to do. Here is what we still need to know: Are there people who are doing this? How would you get the right guidance to achieve this experience?

Is Suzuki describing 1. A deathless, unconditioned state beyond all suffering, or 2. a glimpse of the truth, 3. a high flow state, or 4. a hopeful aspiration passed on for a long time?

DT Suzuki, from his introduction to Herrigel's book:

"One of the most significant features we notice in the practice of archery, and in fact in all the arts as they are studied in Japan and probably also in other Far Eastern countries, is that they are not intended for utilitarian purposes only or for purely aesthetic enjoyments, but are meant to train the mind; indeed to bring it into contact with the ultimate reality…

If one really wishes to be master of an art, technical knowledge is not enough. One has to transcend technique so that the art becomes an "artless art" growing out of the Unconscious."

From Eugen Herrigel's account of his experience of Zen archery in Japan in the 1920's: ···**More than five years went by, and then the Master proposed we pass a test**···

His teacher said: "It is not just a question of demonstrating your skill··· An even higher value is set on the spiritual development of the archer, down to its minutest gesture···"

Herrigel describes the mode of practice set for them: performing the ceremonial steps and postures involved in preparing to shoot and shooting, with special attention to posture, right breathing and deep concentration.

His teacher was teaching them to use the archery "kata" to prepare their body and mind.

Herrigel continues: ···**we began to feel uncommonly concentrated after the first steps**··· the exercises proved so fruitful that we were able to slip effortlessly into the state of "presence of mind." "···We passed the test so successfully··· were awarded diplomas on the spot, each inscribed with the degree of mastery in which we stood···"

This achievement as he describes it in his book, is a good portrait of what is possible in five years of practice in a dojo or range setting. Is this Suzuki's "bringing the mind in contact with the ultimate reality"? Certainly not. But what is it? Is it a pointer? A beginning? But how is the goal realized? Who is doing it? What are they teaching to lead others to the culmination of this path?

I believe that Suzuki's goal here was mainly to show that Zen and Zen budo are accessible to westerners. His frame of reference, like that of other Japanese Zen-budo practitioners, instructors, and their Zen advisors, was the Rinzai school of Zen, one of the three main schools. The examples in the next section of this chapter are familiar to practitioners in this tradition.

D.T. Suzuki and the others give the impression that their view is not merely one frame of reference of many, but that Japanese Rinzai Zen is the culmination of human religious life, the normative standard by which all other religious beliefs, practices and traditions can be measured. This gravity drew Zen and budo together. It has a broad appeal in martial arts.

Zen's "Transformative shock" was transferred to Budo

Joshu's Dog, Joshu's "Mu"

Zen and Zen-budo virtuoso practitioners expressed their "liberation" experience in poetry. Their poems point to a moment of sudden transformation which follows a long period of preparation and the accumulation of propitious causes. The gradual accumulation includes persistent concentration, and training under intense pressure.

This was represented in the *Karate Kid Part 1*, where Daniel, the karate kid, polishes his teacher's car, for a long time, using a precise hand gesture which his teacher showed him. Wax on, wax off. Again, and again. It is difficult, dull, demanding and apparently meaningless. There was a time long ago when people would apply some polish to their cars, by hand, to keep them looking shiny and nice. That is what, on the surface, Mr. Miyagi, the teacher, was asking Daniel to do.

Out of nowhere Mr. Miyagi startles Daniel with a punch. Daniel responds spontaneously blocking the punch, without thought, using exactly the same movement he perfected through the wax-on-wax-off practice. Now the light goes on! – his moment of insight, in action, releases him from confusion about his training, and the legitimacy of his teacher's method. This is not a kensho, but it accords with the traditional Zen budo sudden-insight approach to study, practice, and ultimately, mastery.

This sudden transformation typically is catalyzed by shock – a strike, a paradox, a shout, a sight, a sound – something which evicts the practitioner from their familiar world, disorients them, immediately shuts off analytical thinking, suspending the habits of mind which obstruct and distort fresh, immediate experience.

Like a detonation or an avalanche, this shock releases enormous stored up energy, transforming the practitioner and his world into something altogether new. The first time this happens it is called "kensho," 見性, "seeing one's nature" or "seeing."

For the Zen-budo practitioner, in the ideal case, the shock was the imminence of death, the pressure was battle, and the poetic expression was their death poem, jisei. In this genre the dying warrior maintains complete equanimity and detachment in the presence of death. He is a heroic example to the others called upon to risk their lives in war. Because of his composure at this extreme, in pain, life ebbing away, he can expect to pass through the moment of death without fear, without the negative karma of dying with a mind terrified, confused and clinging.

An example of this motif is presented in Tom Cruise's movie *The Last Samurai*. A character based on General

Saigo Takamori, leader of the last samurai rebellion against the Imperial government, lays dying on the battlefield. He is a warrior, defeated, bleeding, on the threshold of death, his life and his world destroyed by the mechanized military of the new, post-samurai Japan. He has a sudden, vaulting insight into the glorious perfection of the world – a world that once seemed to him corrupt and flawed.

That was the movie version. I mention this and not historical jisei, because it is this movie and others in the Japanese Zen budo genre which have had a strong influence on modern martial arts culture, ideals and practices. The historical jisei have not had so much influence. The Last Samurai screenplay follows the preparation-pressure-shock-enlightenment sequence consistent with the conventions of the Zen and Zen budo tradition.

The first koan in the Mumonkan, the "Gateless Gate" koan collection assembled by the13th century Chinese Ch'an master Wumen Hui-k'ai 無門慧開, presents an example of this use of training, pressure and shock.

In this first koan the practitioner, a student-monk named Joshu, asks his Zen master:

"Does a dog have a Buddha nature?"

No one knows why Joshu asks this. But he seems to have expected a Yes. Maybe his plan was to follow up with another question, investigating the idea of Buddha nature.

A principle in Joshu's Zen tradition holds that every living being has a "Buddha nature" – already existing, already perfect. That intrinsic "Buddha nature" is merely obscured by mental habits of disturbance and confusion. Uncovering one's Buddha nature is the goal and method of practice. This is compared to the clouds parting to reveal the moon. The moon was there all along. Once it was hidden, now you can see it.

So, when Joshu asked his teacher "Does a dog have a Buddha nature?" beginning his Socratic investigation into reality, to Joshu this approach seemed "reasonable." But it was an analytical approach, verboten in what became the Zen tradition. And Joshu had the temerity to try to lead his teacher into a discourse on doctrine. His teacher needed to communicate to Joshu that, in his view, speculative analysis itself is fruitless, deploying concepts and categories which are themselves falsehoods, further obscuring the light of one's own Buddha nature – an avenue of investigation which leads nowhere, leads away from liberative insight, into the endless thicket of speculation and idea.

Joshu was stunned when his teacher shouted:

"Mu!" (Which might simply mean "No!")

What could Joshu say to that?

The answer was paradoxical because while his teacher's answer contradicted fundamental doctrine, Joshu also knew it must be true. His teacher, the living embodiment of the truth, the most important person in the world to him, said so. It was for him shocking, maddening, perplexing.

What Part of "Mu" Do We Not Understand?

But how could it be? There was something Joshu did not understand – but what? Was it about a dog? About Buddha nature? About "having?" Or about "Mu"?

Mu is a Japanese character which indicates negation – it can mean "no" or "is not." It is sometimes used like "un" or "non-" or "-free" in English as in "unlimited" or "non-flammable" or "sugar-free."

As mentioned earlier in the context of the Heart Sutra, understanding "mu" is the insight which opens the door to liberation in this tradition.

Joshu thinks: "But a dog has a Buddha nature, right?" Joshu needed to penetrate this question. To penetrate to the truth which would liberate him forever. This was the truth which would set him free.

(I introduce this theoretical material because it is not just the stages of the development of a practitioner that were adopted by budo from Zen. The objective, the method of practice, the identified obstacles and the means to overcome them, were axiomatic too, as I will show in the budo examples below. And as I mentioned, understanding the use of Mu, i.e., properly understanding the emptiness or no self-nature of objects and of persons, is the essential liberative insight of Mahayana Buddhism, the doctrine and practice world in which Zen grew.)

"Could a dog not have a Buddha nature? How could that be?"

Joshu's teacher told him to go figure it out. For Joshu this became the greatest matter in the universe. This question was the only thing that mattered. He was face to face with it everywhere he looked. He was utterly, heart and soul, day and night, focused on answering this question. Without an answer he was nothing. His life as a practitioner would be wasted. His mission would fail. He would be another lost soul, doomed to drift forever in a sea of suffering, alone. It was completely unbearable. He thought about his teachers' words, his koan. He held it tightly in his heart and mind. He considered it, examined it, dwelled on it, obsessed about it, analyzed it, worked on it and worked on it.

Then he saw through it, in a blinding flash of insight.

Generations of practitioners have since tried to use this same koan in quest of this same result. In fact, Zen master Mumon (he lived in the 13thcentury, 400 years after Joshu) struggled for six years with the "Joshu's Mu" koan, before attaining his kenshō . (Mu is the first character in Mumon's name – 無門 – meaning "No Gate" or "Empty Gate" or "Gateless.")

After his insight had been confirmed by his teacher, Mumon wrote:

> A thunderclap under the clear blue sky
> All beings on earth open their eyes;
> Everything under heaven bows together;
> Mount Sumeru leaps up and dances.

Mumon also said:

> Has a dog Buddha-nature?
> This is the most serious question of all.
> If you say yes or no,
> You lose your own Buddha-nature.

For his descendants Mumon commented:

If you want to pass this barrier, you must work through every bone in your body, through every pore of your skin, filled with this question: What is Mu? and carry it day and night. Do not believe it is the common negative symbol meaning nothing. It is not nothingness, the opposite of existence. If you really want to pass this barrier, you should feel like drinking a hot iron ball that you can neither swallow nor spit out…

(Senzaki/Reps translation)

(In case that doesn't clear it up, for a lucid explanation of the distinction between material non-existence and the Madhyamaka view of emptiness, the doctrinal predicate of Mumon's comment, take a look at the <u>Lam</u>

<u>Rim Chen Mo,</u> Tsongkhapa, Volume 3, chapter 12. The hot iron ball simile is found in the early Buddhist Nikayas.)

The structure of transformation described in these examples, is the same as in all the other examples in Zen and Budo: persistent application of heat and pressure in training, usually catalyzed by shock, yields sudden transformative liberation.

The result is a phase transformation. Properties emerge suddenly which were not present before.

We should note two things about kensho: It occurs in the mind of the practitioner, as fresh insight into how things are.

Karate and Zen: Sogen Sakiyama's Kensho

Sakiyama Sogen, Zen abbot at Kozenji Temple in Shuri, Okinawa, was, for his entire life, a dedicated practitioner of both karate and Zen. He described his kensho to me this way:

"…I went to Enkakuji temple in Kamakura, led by Sogen Asahina Roshi. He was a man of faith, continually praying for the world.

The further you go in practice, the more you discover there is to explore.

Asahina Roshi often hit his disciples very hard, painfully. He was never stingy about it. But there was never a single thought of calculation in it. His whole body and mind were filled with a passion to make something out of his disciples. He radiated intense energy.

One day, after we finished with an important conversation inside Roshi's room, I bowed, preparing to leave. At the moment when I raised my head, suddenly he hit me. I thought my eardrum was broken. At that moment a second blow came. I couldn't understand what happened. My mind went blank.

This was the first time I could really call Asahina Roshi my father from the bottom of my heart. I deeply felt the respect, intimacy and trust implied in the word 'father.'

Roshi, who raised me, departed for the eternal journey less than a month later. It is impossible for me to express my feelings of gratitude toward my late Roshi⋯."

The Rinzai Model for Kensho

Sakiyama Roshi's kensho was a unique event for him but his description is a familiar, traditional one. This is the form followed by Zen-budo practitioners who, like Sakiyama, adopted the Rinzai Zen worldview, values and goals, used its techniques, and shaped their training and understanding to its model.

The Blue Cliff Record is an 11th century koan collection, and is still a primary source of training material in the "Lin Chi" or Rinzai Zen tradition. In the introduction to his translation Thomas Cleary writes:

"…Te Shan (d. 867) was famous for his use of the staff to strike students; Hsueh Feng once had a major insight when struck by Te Shan.

Te Shan's contemporary Lin Chi was equally famous for his shouting…

"the staff of Te Shan and the shout of Lin Chi" is a standard Chan expression to be met frequently in the Blue Cliff Record…" p. xxiii Blue Cliff Record

Zen and Zen influenced Budo use incrementally accumulated pressure followed by sudden shock to produce a phase transformation in advanced practitioners. This change goes beyond the flow-states described in the earlier chapters.

I would ask: What is the nature of the new phase transformation in this tradition? Is this "liberation?" Is the same phase transformation achieved in meditation schools in other traditions? Is it possible to replicate in martial arts training?

Sakiyama did not question his traditions. He embraced them and pursued them wholeheartedly.

Sakiyama's Exhortation

Which explains the shared sense of urgency in Zen and Zen-budo practice, and the vehemence in both traditions with which devotees are encouraged to push themselves beyond normal limits, in practice.

Beyond victory in physical confrontation, Zen-budo teachers like Sakiyama conceive of the real battle as transcendent, extending beyond the concerns of this world to eternity, and believe the stakes to be incomprehensibly high: given that failure to achieve liberation in this life means eons of torment in the future, and in light of the fact that an opportunity to devote ourselves to training – such as we have now – is almost impossible to get.

Once again, here is what he said to me about this. It expresses his view that the goals and methods of Zen and budo are one. I think now it's implications will be clear:

"The essentials of karate-do can only be attained through profound practice. This means that in order to realize what is essential we must experience deep meditation (samadhi.) I am sure you fully understand what I am trying to say. It is most important for us, and for the younger generations, that we cultivate our heart and mind.

"The final hurdle for us is to be free from the limitations of our own ego. The disease of modern people is that they are slaves to money, power, fame, etc. They are enslaved by their own egos, and are unaware of it. You will become a true master when you become aware of it, and become free of it. There is no easy way, but it is the most important task, one worth devoting one's life to accomplishing. This is the central task for anyone trying to master a true martial art.

"As I am writing to you, I can vividly feel your sincerity and passion to pursue this and to master karate-do. 'Do' is an endless and severe way. Therefore, we must endlessly exert ourselves to attain it. How wonderful the 'Do' is!"

Sakiyama Roshi and generations of budo practitioners mapped their path of training on the Zen formulae for practice and liberation, including the primacy of proper form, persistence in practice, and the achievement of spontaneous skillful action through a contentless mind.

Is this their interpretation of the culmination of human achievement, that is of liberation or Buddhahood? This is D.T. Suzuki's claim. It is Musashi's "Emptiness" as expressed in the final chapter of his Book of Five Rings; it is Takuan's claim for mushin, and it is echoed in the Okinawan BuBishi's inclusion of the Kenpo Hakku or "Eight Verses on Karate" conveying the ideal condition of mind as content-free and unobstructed –

> **Harmonize with conditions.**
> **When hands cross have no thought.**

– to be attained in every posture, kata, in kumite, in every moment of life.

Sakiyama expresses his idea of mastery in terms of psychology not Buddhism. He is using the word ego to stand in for a self-centered worldview and for the attachment to self-nature.

When he refers to the "essentials" "attained through profound practice" he is making reference to his karate teacher's motto "Oku Myo Zai Ren Shin" – "Deeply hidden reality arises in training the heart and mind."

This sentence was written in a large shodo, Japanese brush calligraphy, which hung on the wall of his teacher's dojo. He saw it every day during the early years of his karate training. His teacher was Chojun Miyagi, the founder of Goju Ryu. This sentence was also written on one of the two black belts he presented to me.

He presented this to be a constant reminder of the place of practice in a life of meaning and purpose.

The question still remains: Is this liberation? From what? What is the end state like? Bliss and freedom?

But what about all the other people in the world who will live, hurt, suffer and die, who all need help. Do I just get out and leave them? Do I return as a future bodhisattva for endless eons, helping, rescuing, saving, until I have accumulated enough merit and wisdom to be reborn as a fully enlightened Buddha? Is that the goal? But isn't the Buddha here, everywhere? Aren't we already enlightened but don't know it? Those claims are all made.

Is the liberation he is recommending the end of the road? Or is it something provisional, a necessary step? A glimpse of the path ahead, to be continued by practice?

What if the road goes on forever? What if Robert Earl Keen, Jr., J.R.R. Tolkien and the Buddha are correct? Where does Zen's path from kensho take you?

***

Note on "Is it Nirvana?" and "How would you find your way to this experience?" Here is a view from outside the Zen tradition. It is consistent with the doctrinal claims of early Buddhism, but not those of Zen. It is worth reflecting on these views, and the contrasting paths of practice these views imply:

> "The King of Concentrations Sutra" says:
> If you analytically discriminate the lack of self in phenomena
> And if you cultivate that precise analysis in meditation,
> This will cause you to reach the goal, the attainment of nirvana.
> There is no peace through any other cause.

Tsong-Kha-Pa. The Great Treatise On The Stages Of The Path To Enlightenment Vol 3 (Kindle Locations 3908-3909). Kindle Edition; Vol 3 p345 print edition.

***

The Path of Seeing

8th century Indian Buddhist monk Kamalashila, in his STAGES OF MEDITATION, says there is only one way to reach the path of seeing: through the "thorough analysis of the nature of the mind." The Zen tradition concurs with this. But aims to achieve it by different means. Can the practice of martial arts provide the access and the tools to do it? What is the relationship of this "analysis of the nature of the mind" to combative skill development? What about the relationship of the cultivation of bodhicitta to combative skills deployed for the protection of others? If ultimate proficiency and technical mastery is the path to nirvana in Zen budo, what are we to understand about those practitioners who sold their combative skills in professional service for status and pay? Was it only in the genteel, post-war days of the 17th century, when the samurai class was idle, privileged, deprived of purpose, martial challenge and battlefield glory, that the dō ideal, the "martial way" as a path to perfection, presented a compelling, dignified path?

Musashi's Description

Musashi Miyamoto highlights the importance of "Mushin," No-Mind – a flow state, in which an experienced practitioner of martial arts can respond spontaneously to the changing dynamics of a combative encounter, and turn them to advantage, without consciously thinking about them. In his instruction on sword mastery, in the concluding chapter titled "Emptiness", Musashi describes passing through the phase transition boundary into kensho. He says:

"When the clouds of delusion clear away, there is true Emptiness." He says: "Taking emptiness as the way, see the way as emptiness."

He is citing the Buddha-nature assumption that we have an enlightened, perfect nature within us which happens to be covered over by our disturbed condition of mind.

The word he uses for "the way" is "Tao" – "Dō" in Japanese, as in "Karate-Dō".

He is presenting content-free consciousness as 'enlightenment' or as 'seeing emptiness.' This is precisely the Zen view. It is sourced from Lao Tzu, with his emphasis on the inherent value and dynamic potential of vacuity, and is a Taoist understanding of the Buddhist concept of emptiness. The Japanese title Roshi, given to an accomplished Zen master, is pronounced the same way in Japanese as "Lao Tzu" – the name of the legendary founding sage of Taoism.

The descriptions of the sword master's ideal condition of mind mirrors the descriptions of the insight of Zen adepts. Musashi's description of emptiness and of enlightenment differs from the Indo-Tibetan sources' description of the terms "emptiness" and "enlightenment" which use precise definitions – anathema in the Zen tradition. It is not clear what Musashi means by delusion. Zen offers allusions and similes, which in that tradition's view are more genuine than any attempt at a precise, technical definition rendered in language can be. What course of action does that leave aspirants?

Without definitions it is possible to overlook Musashi's omission of the vast range of achievements required for complete liberation in Indo-Tibetan and Chinese Buddhisms, as well as those detailed in the texts and traditions of early Buddhism. Chief among these omissions is a solid grounding in wholesome action. In the classic "ten courses of whole action" which lead upward in spiritual development, the first is "Not taking life." This is one of the vows still taken by lay and ordained people in Zen. All training in spiritual realization in Buddhism from the earliest days, was focused not only on one's own insight, but on assiduously restraining one's harmful behavior – including not stealing, lying, misusing sex, being greedy, harboring ill will toward others – and making effort to treat other people well, being generous to them, patient, and seeking their well-being. Beyond these, in the Mahayana traditions, in which Zen locates itself, the practitioner cultivates a heart full of love and a messianic personal resolve to acquire the skills necessary to work effectively for the happiness and salvation of all living beings. That omission is one reason to suspect that Musashi was presenting a Taoist and Zen version of emptiness – spatial and temporal vacuity and contentless consciousness, in action. And a version of enlightenment which is an inward achievement, bounded by one's own conventionally understood mind and body. But it's hard to tell from here.

In his "Emptiness" chapter he is describing the highest level of warrior skills and virtues. He is said to have defeated sixty opponents in single combat, face to face, at arms-length, using three-foot long, razor-sharp steel blades. In the hands of strong, skilled men, fearless, on fire, hungry for blood and fame, contact was frequently lethal. In Musashi's case only to his challengers. Never to him. He was the undisputed master of his art in his day. His description of his insight, his profound mental and technical mastery of swordsmanship, cuts through the theory and exhortation familiar in the literature.

But he is not talking about total liberation from suffering forever. He did not devote his life to that.

There is a lot of mystification and magical thinking about inner training. Some of it is wishful thinking.

Some of it is tricking the gullible. But genuine inner training is a practical matter, with real technique, real experts and real results. It is not different in that respect from any high-skill pursuit.

By analogy, if you are a surgical resident or a fighter pilot, you will need hands-on experience to really know what you are doing. No one questions that. You cannot just hear about it, read the books or observe your teachers at work. You do need to read the books, know the principles and techniques, and observe experts in action before you go to work. It is obvious that you cannot do top quality surgery as a result of nothing more than sitting quietly and getting intuitive insights from your pre-existing inner surgeon about how to do it, and then whip out your scalpel and, using beginner's mind, deftly "just do it." Has anyone tried to land a fighter jet on a carrier deck, at night, in heavy seas, by just winging it?

Reaching the peak of human potential is not less challenging or technically demanding then this. Like surgery and aviation, it can be done. The consequences of pretending to know what you are doing without actually being trained are disastrous. Generations of monks in ancient times who turned to the "immediate experience" of Zen turned to it after years of theoretical training and experience in practical skills, under the guidance of experts. They were well-prepared for their direct experience.

Ascent in Zen and Budo Require Total Effort

A Zen student called Hsiang-yen met with his teacher Kuei-shan Ling-yu (771-853), who gave him a koan to work on. He worked on it for a long time but he was unable to understand it. It was too much. He quit.

He wandered away from his monastery and walked until he found himself at a place which he could see was a sacred site. It was the shrine which marked the grave of the Sixth Patriarch of Chinese Zen, Hui-neng. He decided to stay. He became a groundskeeper, sweeping the fallen leaves from the paths of the temple.

Day in and day out Hsiang-yen swept the paths. He thought about nothing but sweeping. One day, after hours of monotonous rhythmic sweeping, his broom launched a pebble into a bamboo grove next to the shrine. The pebble smacked into a piece of hollow bamboo and went "Clunk!".

The sound shocked him. His mind went blank. He said,

"One clunk! I have forgotten everything!"

He wrote:

"Last year's emptiness was not true emptiness,
this year even the wind can get through."

Hsiang-yen, according to the Zen tradition, was "enlightened."

This is the way Japanese Rinzai Zen and Zen-budo understand the relationship of long, dedicated practice to sudden transformation – as a phase-transition. The content of the practice is not standardized. For Zen and Zen budo the cessation of mental content itself is liberative. It is considered liberative because the cessation of perceptible cognitive activity is taken to be the immediate experience of "emptiness." It frequently occurs with senses engaged – not withdrawn in meditation as in other Buddhist traditions.

The depth of this experience can be profound and transformative and good. A sudden openness of perspective, a sudden relief from the confinement of a habitual view of one's self as separate from everything, at the center of the universe, with the world unpredictable, always uneasy, is a wonderful feeling. It is a legitimate experience. It is also fleeting.

Is it liberation from sickness, old age and death? Is it freedom from craving, ignorance and suffering? Those are the right questions to ask. And if the tradition, or the present-time exponents of it, wave those questions away as irrelevant, inappropriate, based in speculative views unrelated to real experience, or coming up because you or I or another interlocutor, sincere as we may be, are too suspicious, too dumb, too corrupt, too rigid, or too lazy, or too disloyal to get it – then we ought to consider the possibility that they do not know.

We need not infer from that that no one knows. The acceptance of the validity of this kind of Zen enlightenment experience as liberative, and the expectation that this form of insight experience will arise under pressure, were transferred from Zen to budo practice in the dojo, and to the battlefield.

Takuan's Description

In a letter written by 16th century Japanese Zen master Takuan Soho to his disciple and client, sword master Munenori Yagyu, called "The Mysterious Record of Immoveable Wisdom" there is a section called "The Affliction of Abiding in Ignorance." The title refers to the central matter in all these Zen and Zen-budo examples – removing the mental disturbances which distort our view, and trap us in an unenlightened state.

In his advice Takuan applies the Zen understanding of liberation to sword fighting. He says:

"In the practice of Buddhism, there are said to be fifty-two stages, and within these fifty-two, the place where the mind stops at one thing is called the abiding place. Abiding signifies stopping, and stopping the mind is being detained in some matter, which may be any matter at all.

To speak in terms of your own martial art, when you first notice that the sword is moving to strike you, if you think of meeting that sword just as it is, your mind will stop at the sword in just that position, your own movements will be undone, and you will be cut down by your opponent. This is what stopping means.

– translated by Thomas Cleary

The "52 stages" seems to be a reference to the Gandavyuha Chapter of the Kegon Kyo, the Flower Ornament Sutra collection. It is a description of the vast path to enlightenment along which the seeker proceeds without stopping, to reach the ultimate goal. the seeker meets 52 teachers, passes through 52 stages of transformation, overcoming 52 mental obstacles, until completing the path to Nirvana.

The title of this chapter in English is "Entry into the Realm of Reality." The "realm of reality" is a name for nirvana.

Todai-ji temple, the old center of Kegon Buddhism in Japan, has a strong tantric tradition, including the veneration of fierce guardian deities – the same pantheon which is central to ritual life at the Shaolin Temple in Henan, China. Shaolin was the legendary site of Bodhidharma's Buddhist mission to China from India, and in fact was a fortified citadel for centuries. Its military reputation was preeminent at one time, and its military contribution to the Yuan empire led emperor

Kublai Khan to designate Shaolin the head temple for all of Buddhism in China.

In his introductory line Takuan makes a connection to the Buddhist warrior tradition, indicating to his military client that his Buddhist teaching is lofty and complete and has a formidable martial legacy.

Then he moves to technique: Takuan knows that danger in battle comes when changing conditions outpace your ability to adapt and respond to them. In fact, there is no way you can simply respond to your enemy's actions and prevail. Warriors need to take the initiative and get ahead of their opponent's action cycle, in order to win. Anyone with experience knows you cannot do that if your mind is "abiding" i.e., getting stuck, anywhere, in the fleeting permutations of combatives, which change by the time you respond.

In training as a sniper or for hostage rescue, using simulation rounds and role players, or high-tech, interactive 360° video simulation environments, operators learn to respond "without abiding", without second-guessing, without anticipation or hesitation, with the near-instantaneous compression of observation, interpretation, shoot/no-shoot decision-making, and action. Innocent lives are in jeopardy. Your life is exposed. Your job is to save the innocent, rescue the hostage and capture the enemy if you can. The ones who can achieve this with no errors stay on the team. All the participants learn from it. And in real life, outside the dojo, outside the simulation, when you apply these skills, the enemy will be moving, may be undetected, and is now, or soon will be, shooting at you.

To "stop" even for an instant is to be destroyed. How can you get out ahead of your opponent's action cycle?

That is the question Takuan is answering. He is using Zen analysis of mind and phenomena to prescribe the remedy for this perennial tactical problem.

Takuan's emphasis is on the paramount importance of an "empty" mind. As mentioned earlier, Takuan said:

"No-mind is the same as right mind. It neither hardens nor remains static. It is called no-mind when the mind

has neither discrimination nor a single thought, but moves unimpeded through the whole body and extends through the entire self… The no-mind is placed nowhere. Yet it is not like wood or stone… When this no-mind has been well-developed the mind does not come to rest on one thing nor does it miss anything…."

Compare this "no-mind" with the high flow states of Musashi, which push against the boundary crossed by the kensho insights of Joshu, Hsiang-yen and the pebble, Sakiyama's double-slap kensho, and the others.

This insight, this open condition of mind, unattached to fixed forms, plans or characteristics, this liberation from "abiding" or getting stuck, is what Takuan is describing and recommending to his warrior disciple and patron.

From a combatives standpoint, this is an accurate diagnosis of the problem and prescription to remedy it. However, Takuan makes the claim that this is not only effective for maximum performance, but that it is an 'enlightened' state of mind – the consummate human achievement, as a result of which the practitioner is completely 'liberated.'

What does he mean?

In the examples above we have seen people push against this boundary. We have seen that a sudden shock, applied at the perfect moment, to the consummately prepared practitioner, catalyzes the change. Like an avalanche when the last snowflake lands and the whole mountainside collapses.

Is this kind of transformation possible from martial arts? That is the claim. That is certainly different from "just doing it" or being an innocent beginner with no concepts, using "beginner's mind" to surpass the adept. It is different from entering a high-performance flow state, like Eugen Herrigel, like all of us, after a few years of good, consistent training.

If this great transformation is possible through martial arts, it will require total preparation for the decisive moment. But in this tradition, what constitutes proper preparation? What is "total?"

This story first appeared in Chinese Zen lore about 1,000 CE – about 1,500 years after the Buddha taught the gradual path to nirvana in India, 500 years after Bodhidharma brought the Mahayana Lankavatara Sutra to China. By this time some sects had become large, land-owning, state-supported institutions.

Which, like so many religious institutions in all traditions, was seen by some as having codified a once vibrant spiritual path, dried out and hardened into a conveyor of nothing more than dogmatic formulae. Legend has it that Zen was born to bring practice back to life.

Kata and the Diamond Sutra Master

I want to tell you about something happened a thousand years ago, in Sichuan province, China. At the center of this story was an extraordinary scholar. He was a master of the Diamond Cutter Sutra. He could recite the sutra without hesitation or flaw.

It ran through his mind ceaselessly. He could quote the relevant passages of the commentaries, paragraphs at a time. He knew from a phrase where the debate might lead, how the arguments were framed, and how they could be contested.

For him this book changed everything. It was as mysterious as the sky, endlessly open. A vast ocean he traveled, navigating star to star. He would discover new worlds. He would discover a new one right here.

As the story begins, he was walking. He had been walking for days. It was hot. It had a long way to travel to the capital.

On his back he carried a little library. Every evening when he stopped to rest, he studied.

He was on his way to the great debate. The emperor would preside. The emperor would choose the victor.

Great scholars from everywhere would contend.

This year he would challenge them.

He could see it.

He was ready.

He would enter the circle of great scholars.

He would be consulted by the powerful,

valued by the wise.

But at the moment his mouth was dry, his collar was wet, his back was sore.

He saw a little tea shop, tucked in a bend in the road.

He entered the courtyard. He set his books down near a small, square table.

An elderly woman came out from the shop. She greeted him with a bow and cool drink.

He was covered in dust, but he wore the clothes of a scholar.

He took the cup of water with two hands, drank it all, feeling the cool water soothe his throat, he thanked her.

Breathing deeply, his exhaustion lifting, he asked her for a cup of tea.

"I need to refresh my mind," he told her.

She smiled, and nodded and turned to get his tea.

Then she stopped and turned back toward him.

Sir, are you a scholar?

Yes, I am, he said.

What do you study?

The Diamond Cutter – the Vajracchedika Prajnaparamita Sutra, he said.

I see, said the old woman… Before I get your tea, I would like to ask you a question…

Of course, grandmother.

The Diamond Sutra says that the mind of the past is gone and ungraspable, is that right?

Yes, that's right, said the scholar.

And the mind of the future does not yet exist, so it too is ungraspable.

Yes, that's right, he said.

And according to the Sutra, the present mind cannot be grasped either. Is that right?

Yes, you really know the sutra well, he said. He smiled kindly at the simple, pious old woman.

She was motionless.

She held him with her gaze as she asked: Then sir, which mind is it that you would like to refresh?

With this he was stunned. A chill took hold of him. He could not answer.

In his shock

the world stood still

and began to open as he searched for an answer.

Then the dawn broke. The world became clear.

A freedom that resembled nothing he had experienced before opened his heart and opened the prison of his mind. The world became brilliant.

The plain, serene face of the tea lady vanished, as she went to get his tea.

He drank it.

They say that next he abandoned his books, gave up his life of scholarship, and turned from the path of study to the path of training.

In modern times people misunderstood this story. Some thought the story showed that study was useless. They missed the point.

At the pivotal moment the monk saw directly, the truth that his scholarly study was pointing to all along. He suddenly saw that by attending rigidly to the words, to the description of reality, he missed the experience of the reality to which those words pointed.

His training worked. His mind was well-prepared. His teacher, the tea lady, skillfully catalyzed his insight and transformation.

This story does not reject knowledge and study. It views them as a necessary step, to master and to leave behind.

That is consistent with the Buddha's teaching that practice and study are to be used as a raft, to cross the river of craving and ignorance, to be left behind upon reaching the other shore.

The path of the Zen master in east Asian lore, as expressed in this story, maps to the path of the master of Japanese Zen-budo.

The martial arts parallel to scholarship is found in the study of kata. If we treat the kata as objects with magic powers, which can confer mastery just by memorizing them, then they will fail in their purpose.

If we recognize the kata as instrumental, learn them, investigate them, practice them wholeheartedly, then, when they have done their job, when we have used them to shape and transform our body and mind, we can be done with them. But we cannot do without them.

John Boyd's "Independent Action"

United States Air Force Colonel John Boyd was a fighter pilot and aircraft designer. He performed at an incomprehensible level of achievement which has not been surpassed. He may be the most influential military theorist of the modern era. His insights on the nature of time, space and mind in combat match Takuan's and Yagyu's, whose ideas he studied.

Boyd's theoretical work is the basis of warfighting doctrines of militaries around the world. It has informed the primary combat doctrine of the US Marines.

He was faced with the same tactical problems in the arena of fighter aviation as the samurai faced in sword fighting. He solved them in the same way, although he expressed them differently. This is directly relevant to us as martial artists, but its relevance is much broader than that, as he reflects on issues which we all face, regardless of time, place or culture.

We can view Boyd's insights in light of what we know about Zen budo's prescription for tactical combatives.

One of Boyd's insights is known by the acronym "OODA," which describes the sequence of a combatant's perception, thought and behavior in the battlespace. Boyd noticed that under pressure, combatants – pilots, fighters, competitors in any space – will enter into continuous cycles of engagement in which they Observe, Orient, Decide and Act, again and again. Each cycle changes the operating conditions, and requires a fresh response.

The sequence is fast. At high levels of performance, it occurs faster than conscious perception, will or cognition. Making good use of this is only achievable by intensive preparation through training.

Harry Hillaker, chief designer of the F-16, said of Boyd's OODA theory:

"Time is the dominant parameter. The pilot who goes through the OODA cycle in the shortest time prevails because his opponent is caught responding to situations that have already changed⋯."

⋯ The key to survival and autonomy is the ability to adapt to change, not perfect adaptation to existing circumstances. Indeed, Boyd noted that radical uncertainty is a necessary precondition of physical and mental vitality: all new opportunities and ideas spring from some mismatch between reality and ideas about it ⋯"

This description applies to sword-fighting or kumite as well as to combat aviation.

Boyd, in his two written works: "Patterns of Conflict" and "Destruction and Creation," uses the term "independent action" to describe the pilot's optimal mind state. He seems to use this to mean what Takuan meant by "unfettered mind" and "immovable mind." In some ways it resembles the meditative achievement known by the technical term "pliancy" (prasrabhi in Sanskrit) – unobstructed freedom of movement in mind and body. Tibetan Buddhist author Sogyal Rinpoche defined pliancy using the phrase "riding your mind," and compared it to riding a horse you have tamed and trained well.

Since the problems of combatives presented in medieval Japan and in modern warfare are in many ways identical, it is no surprise that the solutions are as well. In both cases these are solutions that reflect insight into practical applications of metaphysical truths. These are not religious insights per se, although religions address them. The deep metaphysical truth I am referring to – functioning at a level deeper than what we ordinarily notice – is that things change, rapidly and continually, that individuals cannot act unilaterally but only within a constellation of causes, conditions and effects which are themselves continually transforming and making fresh demands, that the mind gets stuck as the world moves on, and that events naturally outpace perception. Takuan noticed and Boyd noticed, and we can notice it too.

These insights and experiences all fall within the realm of Flow or Mushin. They are consistent with the insights produced through the Japanese Zen-budo experience, framed in the Rinzai Zen worldview. These are at the high end of the experience of Flow. But the experiences which Boyd, Takuan, and Yagyu are describing remain contingent conditions of mind and body. They are temporary. They do not offer liberation from suffering or confusion, certainly not for all beings. They do not address this matter.

Boyd, a tactical and theoretical genius, a performer of the highest caliber, evincing consummate mastery, performing at the highest possible level of achievement of a warrior in his field of action, showing stunning integrity in a corrupt world, was brilliant, accomplished and admirable, self-centered and a disturber of the peace. He had glimpses into the nature of reality. He worked hard. He did not work on the issue of liberation from suffering. Liberation does not spring inevitably from skill mastery.

Where do we find the access point to the deepest experience? Where is the gateway to the realm beyond mushin or flow, beyond kensho to satori? Martial artists claim you can pass through this gateway through the practice of martial arts. Modern martial artists – in books, on websites, in videos – talk about self-realization, your true nature, true reality and so on. What are they talking about? Do they know? Are they holding this ideal out before their students as an incentive to practice? Is this the way they use it themselves? Can this promise be fulfilled through the practice of martial arts?

I probed the Zen-budo literature and met with practitioners. I investigated how I could follow its recommended path through to the end. I did not let the kettle cool. I did as my teachers recommended. I found deep training, good insights, good friends, deepening mastery of technique. At the same time, I encountered limits to liberation through martial arts practice which do not appear in the lore and literature of martial arts.

Zen-budo borrowed some ideas and techniques from Buddhism, selecting ones that enabled the development of precise and powerful mental focus and high states of flow. These found a realm of applicability in the cultures of east Asia, including martial cultures, as they have in the modern world. This selective appropriation of some Buddhist tools excluded many others. Some of the ones which were not included are more potent, more valuable and more difficult to use than the one's which were adopted by martial artists.

We are not stuck with that. We are building on the work that has been done.

I mentioned that Indian scholar Kamalashila in his STAGES OF MEDITATION said the one way to reach the path of seeing, kensho, is through the "thorough analysis of the nature of the mind." Difficult, arduous, essential, and rarely done. He says this is necessary to reach kensho, the Heart Sutra's path of seeing, "sotapanna" or stream entry in the terminology of the southern tradition. That is point one. Point two: Nowhere does Kamalashila say that this is sufficient for liberation.

In the thermodynamic phase-transition model, when energy was added, ice melted, and the water flowed. As it got warmer the water became turbulent, and then reached its boiling point. The water received enough energy to transcend what appeared to be fixed, inherent properties. At kensho, we might say, vapor is escaping, rising, moving freely. In the traditional presentation, kensho is not reversible. It will need deepening and stabilizing. There will be errors in perception and disturbances in mind, but after kensho the practitioner will recognize these errors, and proceed with energy toward full enlightenment. In the case of practitioners whose realization falls short of kensho, this analogy is apt in another respect: the vapor state, although energetic, is temporary, subject to conditions. When conditions change, when the temperature cools, the steam will condense, becoming water once again. A deep experience, an exalted one, even a life-changing one, may not be liberation.

***

Ansei Ueshiro's Nin Tai

It is hard to trace the network of influences that touch us. They propagate undetected, like bamboo, shoots and runners traveling underground, appearing unexpectedly, at a distance. The tradition continues.

One day Ansei Ueshiro walked onto the training floor. This was the first time I had seen him there in my three years in the dojo. I had met him briefly several times over the years. Those of us who started in the 1980's had never seen him do karate.

Mr. Ueshiro was an early Okinawan importer of Shorin Ryu to the US, arriving in the early 60's from Okinawa, as an emissary from the dojo of Shoshin Nagamine. Ueshiro developed a group in the New York area. Within a few years he was no longer associated with Shoshin Nagamine, but he retained an enthusiastic following in the USA.

One person asked him if he still trained. He said "24 hours a day."

We had all heard about him. We heard that his fingers were blown off when he was a boy, playing with unexploded munitions in a field in Okinawa, after the war. We heard that he was extremely tough, unpredictable, and hard to read.

So, when he appeared in the dojo, and walked through our group of black belts one day in the mid 80's, it created a stir.

He said a few words of greeting and then, opening a large folder set against the wall, he handed three "shodo" pieces – hand-brushed kanji – to three people. Two of them were small, card sized pieces, which he gave to two of the long-time black belts. They were pleased and honored to receive these gifts. He gave the third one, a big framed piece, to me. I thought this was strange, and everyone agreed. People considered him inscrutable. This confirmed it.

It was strange partly because I did not know him. There were people in the room who knew him well; some had been training in his group for years. I was a new black belt with no particular role or status in the dojo. But there it was, he handed me this expertly brushed, professionally framed calligraphy of the characters "Nin Tai."

It looked beautiful to me. But I did not know what it said. He told me what it said in Japanese, which I also did not understand.

Soon I found out a little bit about what it meant. It seemed to be an encouragement, a push in the right direction.

I was training at the dojo every day. The city at that time was in decline and the streets were perilous. Muggings were common. Stepping over people, dead or drugged or passed out, lying on the sidewalk, was part of everyday life.

My work environment was high pressure. I was wound tight, and was training like crazy. I was competitive. Which may be why he gave me the Nin Tai. He appreciated my dedication. But he may have been telling me to direct it in a positive way.

In martial arts you may hear: **"Nin means 'endurance' and Tai means to 'withstand and resist.' Together they connote perseverance under the harshest conditions."**

Traditionally the expression Nin Tai refers to the third of the Buddhist "Six Perfections": the "Perfection of Patience." 忍耐力の完璧さ – Nintai-ryoku no kanpeki-sa.

The "Perfection of Patience" is sometimes defined simply as not getting angry. But it does not imply putting up with everything, or being passive.

Nin Tai is described this way:

"1. Disregarding harm done to you, 2. Accepting the suffering arising in your mind stream, 3. Being certain about the teachings and firmly maintaining belief in them. There are three sets of factors incompatible with these: for the first, hostility; for the second, hostility and loss of courage; and for the third, disbelief and dislike. Perfecting patience (Nin Tai) means that you simply complete your conditioning to a state of mind wherein you have stopped your anger and the like…" (-Lam Rim Chen Mo, Tsong Kha Pa, Vol 2, Ch12, p1; published by Snow Lion)

Traditionally the "Perfection of Patience" is coupled with the fourth perfection: the "Perfection of Effort." This union makes patient endurance active, not passive.

If that is what Ansei Ueshiro was saying with his gift then it was insightful and practical advice – much needed at the time. The fact that it took me years to grasp it's meaning is no fault of his. My impression now, many years later, is that he was teaching me something, and at the same time, teaching everyone else present: that in a dojo, as in your own life, it is better to redirect excessive energy in a positive direction, than to tolerate it, waste it, obstruct it or stifle it.

One day, a few years after Ueshiro's Nin Tai presentation, my phone rang. Ansei Ueshiro was on the other end. He had never called me before. But he said he wanted to offer me the use of one of his company's delivery trucks, as I was moving away to set up my own dojo. This was generous of him.

When he said he trained "24 hours a day" I did not think much of it. Maybe it was swagger, or evasion, or something he told himself – because he was not training karate by then. But now I think, maybe not. Continual practice is real.

In the Eastern Church people pray the Jesus Prayer, ten or 12 words long, all day, as a continual practice. The older generation of Tibetan women, a world away from their homes, repeat the six-syllable mantra continually, while walking, working waiting, setting up, clearing away. Maybe this brings them home, no matter where they are. Dedicated aspirants in every tradition I know of continually return their minds to practice, while eating, falling asleep, waking up, anytime their attention is not needed elsewhere, to keep their mind healthy, focused on the wholesome, reminded of the sacred, not allowing their hearts to be invaded by the profane or seduced by the trivial.

I did not know Ansei Ueshiro beyond our few, brief meetings. I never saw his karate. But he did inspire many people to train, including, indirectly, me. I appreciate that it was his influence that got me started in this style, whose power I spotted instantly. I appreciate his timely Nin Tai advice, and his 24-hour practice. None of us knows what effect we may have. His influence continues.

***

Doctrines of Liberation

With Senses Engaged

The observation that in the Zen tradition the moment of liberative insight occurs "with senses engaged" is not trivial. It is distinct from the main stream of the Buddhist tradition. The Buddha taught that when the sense organ, sense consciousness and sense object meet this produces "contact" a key component in the causal nexus called dependent origination which accounts for our being bound in samsara – the cycle or vortex of pleasures and pains, dissatisfaction, difficulties and death.

Withdrawing the senses in meditation is therefore conducive to liberative practice. By the time Zen – in China called the Ch'an school – arose, older schools of Buddhism were seen by some as having fossilized into institutionalized conveyors of dogma, no longer capable of vital transformative spiritual nourishment and liberative training. The Ch'an schools' soteriological method and theory were intended to challenge the conventional wisdom of their time.

There is a precedent for "sudden" insight with senses engaged in early Buddhism. There are instances recorded in the sutras when the Buddha, recognizing the ripeness of the mind of a visitor, gave the perfect teaching to produce transformative insight in the mind of that visitor. Two special factors account for this: the unique capacity of a fully enlightened Buddha to see into the mind of his visitor, and the mind of the visitor being thoroughly prepared in past lives, acquiring collections of merit and wisdom sufficient to be receptive to the catalyzing words of the Buddha.

It is worth considering whether these two versions of this motif – the Zen version and the early Buddhist version – are communicating the same understanding of sudden enlightenment.

The Human Buddha becomes the Transcendent Buddha

There were doctrinal changes which account for this change. The later Chinese Buddhist Ch'an tradition had an understanding of the Buddha which differed from the early Buddhist view.

In early Buddhism the core texts for teaching doctrine and practice were the words of the historical Buddha, the sutras, and some early commentaries.

The Buddha's human presence, as a teacher, was understood as a unique and pivotal event in this eon, one of paramount importance, making it possible to relieve the endless suffering of this world, which before his appearance in this world, his enlightenment and his 45-year teaching mission, had been impossible.

By the time of the rise of Ch'an it was the cosmic aspect of the Buddha which was central to doctrine and devotion. The texts that devotees studied were not the words of the historical Buddha, but literature which first appeared centuries later.

Maybe the change came about in response to a yearning for the immediate presence of the enlightened teacher, the source of wisdom and love. Maybe it was due to the influence of universalist doctrines in Chinese Taoist thought. Maybe it was in response to the limits of the human mind: since it is not possible for us to comprehend the infinite, we have difficulty rationalizing the relationship between the human and the divine or universal. This is an issue in religious, philosophical and scientific exploration.

The new vision of the cosmic Buddha meant that the vast world and all the things in it are the Buddha, that the Buddha is always present, everywhere.

Thus, with the right condition of mind, with deep penetration of the truth by means of proper cultivation, one could come face to face with the Buddha anytime, anywhere. In every moment one was, in Zen doctrine, manifesting the Buddha or face to face with the Buddha – sometimes in the guise of your Zen master, but also as a pebble hitting a tile, in the mountains and rivers, everywhere your mind could go – and receiving endless teachings from him.

(For more on this transition see On Being Buddha, *by Paul J. Griffiths.)*

This is a critical point. The way the Zen budo school accounts for sudden enlightenment during training, or even in battle, with senses engaged and the body in action, is through the imminence of the cosmic Buddha and our own Buddha nature.

An expression of this, from 13th century Zen master Dogen's *"Genjokoan":*

"To study the Way is to study the self. To study the self is to forget the self. To forget the self is to be enlightened by all things."

The preparation of the mind for this encounter with the cosmic, imminent Buddha is done by emptying it, as seen in the Zen budo examples above.

The Early Buddhist Approach

This is distinct from the early Buddhist approach to preparing the mind. There were many techniques but the theme was to rid the mind of the five hindrances: sense desire, ill-will, laziness, restlessness, and doubt; and develop the seven factors of enlightenment: mindfulness, investigation of the nature of reality, energy, joy, tranquility, concentration and equanimity. On this basis wisdom practice into impermanence, unsatisfactoriness, and no-self nature will lead to breakthrough and ultimately to liberation in nirvana. This stream of practice is still in use.

The Zen We Met

My intention in this examination is not to disparage Zen or Zen practitioners.

It is to discover an effective way to use our dojo practice optimally and see if it is possible to go beyond the limits of convention to fulfill the promise of ultimacy claimed in the east Asian martial traditions.

A point worth considering whether, after another thousand years, some of the Zen schools, with their long history of support from the military governments which ruled Japan, may also have to some degree themselves declined into promotion of dogmatic absolutism, observance of ritual form, and fealty to worldly interests. And that this transformation may have been undetected by the eager but unprepared foreigners who embraced the spare aesthetic, habit of self-regard, post-modern devaluation of language, mystification of the Zen master, bells, chants and incense, formal zendo etiquette, the exotic clothes and hairstyles – while never knowing the doctrinal apparatus that Zen was long ago created to revive. Or the seriousness of purpose which the apparatus was devised to embody. It is possible.

Thich Nhat Hanh, the influential Vietnamese Zen monk, thinker and writer, said that it was a shame that the Japanese government, in the 1870's, decreed that Zen monks could marry.

Eventually almost all did. This removed them from the vows that shaped the lives of Buddhist monastics for 2,500 years, and instead directed their attention to family, politics, and other worldly concerns. It was a time when a zealous demonstration of nationalism reassured the Japanese nation that the Zen institutions were loyal. The Japanese Zen institution ardently supported the Imperial conquests of the early- and mid-20th century. (See Zen at War, Brian Victoria.) There was more to Zen than this, but the importers of Zen to the west were trained during this period, and carried old assumptions and new ambitions with them.

Thich Nhat Hanh respected the people he was speaking to and the long tradition he was speaking about. But he did not refrain from giving guidance where he thought it would be useful.

The same was true for Sakiyama Roshi. His teaching style was forceful and direct, a real old-time Zen master. What he approved was single-minded focus, with the mind, the will and the body focused on a single point. His approval might be a word, a look, a gesture. It could come at any time – while the trainee was lighting incense, ringing a bell, taking a seat, speaking.

It was not aggression or even assertiveness he was responding to, it was clarity, purpose and focus. He would rebuke the opposite. He had no patience for theorizing, distraction or half-heartedness. He was blunt and devoted. People appreciated him. This way of teaching reflected his martial arts and his martial arts were cultivated on the foundation of his Zen training.

What he taught, as far as I experienced it, was form and mind united in purposeful action in the present moment. The Zen ideal. Indispensable for budo. Full commitment, in a flow state.

He was highly accomplished. The fact that he responded so intensely to my short essay that he titled True Karate Dō, showed several things. That he strongly felt the need to connect dojo practice with genuine spiritual cultivation. That spiritual cultivation was not just development of a deep flow state but based in sound conduct: being generous to others, not getting angry, developing moral restraint and ethical action, and on that basis to use the flow state as the platform for penetrating wisdom. That program is what was in my piece and what moved him. That is what I felt was essential for dojo practice and for wholesome Zen practice.

What I was recommending in that essay, the reason I wrote it and was determined to embark in the direction it set, was that my vision was at odds with what I had experienced in dojos and the Zen Centers in the US. I was recommending something new – although it was not my personal recommendation at all, and it was not new, and it was not something I was able to accomplish. It was a concise presentation of the Mahayana tradition's ideal behaviors and path to perfection.

That this was news, that it moved him so much that he shared it and advocated it within the karate community on Okinawa showed how thoroughly Zen had dispensed with the core Mahayana doctrines. It showed, by Sakiyama's embrace of these ideas, considering his experience in the zendo and the dojo, in teaching Zen and Okinawan karate around the world, how much he agreed that these ideas were needed to bring practice to life.

It was also significant that when I said that it would benefit dojo training to take all these seriously, that the concern with service, with treating people decently, behaving with restraint and dignity should be part of training, that these were a necessary crucible for good technical practice, and were as necessary as a focused body, mind and will, he rejected this as heterodoxy. It was too radical for him. That was the end of that.

Religious tools have been clipped out of the context of spiritual aspiration and appropriated for worldly aims. They are powerful tools. They work. They have produced spectacular results. They have also caused trouble.

Steve Jobs was devoted to Zen. The following was written by Koyama Tetsuya and published in English on nippon.com in 2016:

> To get a fresh perspective on Steve Jobs and Zen, I talked with Yamashita Ryōdō, one of the most influential spiritual figures in Japan today. From his headquarters in Kamakura, Yamashita travels globally, providing instruction and guidance in meditation to students all over the world, including the United States…

Yamashita believes that Zen informed Steve Jobs's unique and spectacularly successful approach to product development.

"He didn't do any kind of marketing research," notes Yamashita.

"Through his practice of *zazen*, he went deep inside to see more clearly what he wanted himself. The things he made resonated deeply with others precisely because they came from a place deep inside himself. For him, the ultimate marketing research tool was discovering what exactly he himself really wanted."

Like Musashi, like John Boyd, worldly, intensely focused, the center of his own universe, with complete unity of action through his life. Which is only possible in a high flow state. What he wanted seems to have had nothing to do with health, happiness, virtue or spiritual liberation.

Jobs, like Boyd, Takuan, Yagyu, and Musashi, were immensely focused, powerful, brilliant people. They were professionals. The effects of what they valued, and what they did ripple out through the world.

Meditation does not make you a better person. It can make you a worse person. It depends on what you meditate on - what mental habits you create. That is why we cultivate benevolence, restraint of impulse and responsibility toward others. Martial arts works the same way, as Sakiyama saw.

If we overlook this then we remain self-centered, seeking advantage for ourselves only. Then as we meditate or train, we reinforce those pre-existing mental habits. We can easily become more selfish, more greedy and more grandiose. That is what happened as unprepared people launched their careers as masters.

Sakiyama approved intense focus and total, unified commitment to the moment of action, in karate and in spiritual life. He spent a lifetime mastering those. It is powerful, hard to accomplish.

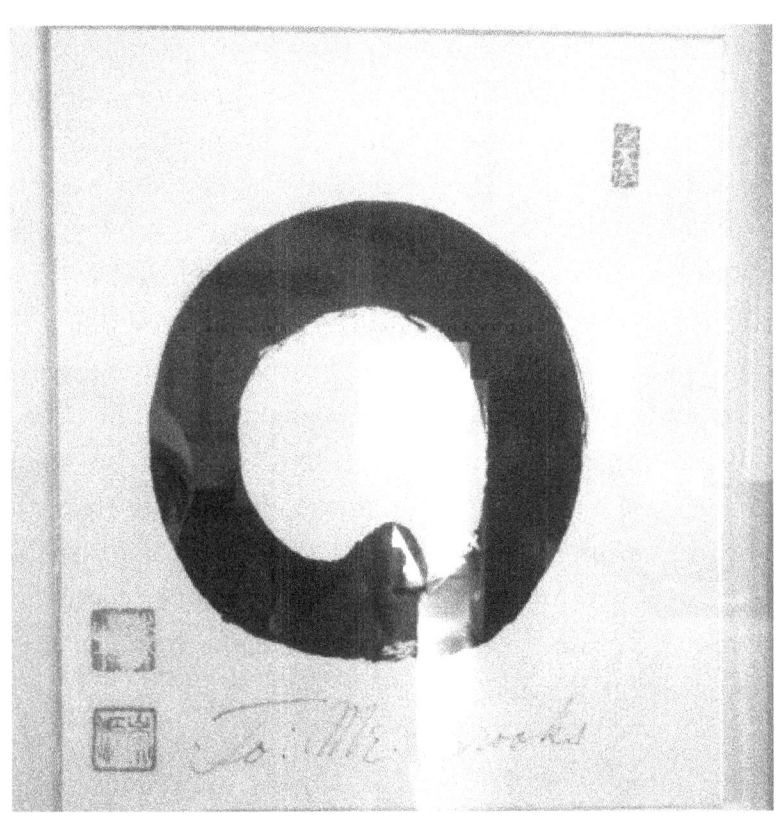

Enso
shodo by Sakiyama Sogen,
from the collection of the Enso Theater, Portland, OR

The Enso, like Mu, represented a key object of contemplation leading to insight and liberation, referred to by the words "no self-nature" or "emptiness." This is accepted as a mystifying idea. But you and your parents and your children and probably almost everyone you know learned to count to ten. You memorized it. You learned to write it down. Little by little, it became natural. It is unlikely that anyone, as they were scratching out their little numbers on their lined notebook paper, or even typing them out on their devices, ever wrote 8, 9, 10, and as they wrote that last one-zero stopped and flipped out and said that zero is completely inscrutable and ineffable and other worldly! I doubt it. Because it is easy to see that the zero just says something that could be here is not here.

The Romans were great and powerful. They built buildings that have lasted thousands of years with advanced building technologies that were not understood until very recently. There was a gladius and aegis for everyone who wanted one. There was law and language and leadership. But they didn't have nothing. Not in the numbering system anyway.

Calculating all the wealth rolling into the capitol was cumbersome.

It seemed to take almost as long to count your stake as it did to purloin it, relying on a checkerboard table, using a kind of abacus technique to count rows and columns of tokens. Just ask the Chancellor of the Exchequer how his department got its name. And ask how much easier things got once Roman influence waned, and an innovation arrived in Britain, unexpected, an ancient Indian representation of nullity, "sunnya", officially christened an Arabic numeral by this time, which made its way around the world with commerce, trade and conquest.

The zero made everything add up. The zero made it a snap, recently, to change from billions to trillions as a common unit of public discourse. That was nothing. It is not that the Enso just looks like a zero. It is a zero. The ancient Indian philosophers and the ancient Indian mathematicians hit the same nail on the head. Those tantalizing, elegant, artful, allusive Zen circles are zeros.

To know this idea is not the same as seeing the nature of reality, what the symbol points to, directly. That takes training and practice.

To scrutinize phenomena, searching for what we presume to be there but in fact is not there, is facilitated by reason, not impeded by it. The alternative to knowing what you are looking for, what you are examining, and how to do it, may be spending your life sitting on a cushion and getting relatively nothing.

Satisfaction on an Autumn Evening

All this philosophy provides insight into fighting, meditating and religion, but those realms are not its main concern. The people from all walks of life who grappled with these ideas and who tried to practice the ideals derived from them, were making an attempt to crack the code of reality.

The idea was and is, that if you can get it right, if you can actually understand what is going on and how it works, you can stop making foolish mistakes, stop getting frustrated, stop getting hurt and confused, stop causing trouble, and be free of the burdens, yearning and remorse that encumber our lives.

The warriors did this. The monks did it. The emperors and the artists and the artisans did it too. Farmers and merchants, beggars and kings found themselves in the same boat. The guys in suits who I meditated with early every morning on Okinawa, before they headed off to the office, were up to the same thing. They had a compass they used to orient to life, to create a path, and to follow it. Not everyone has one.

It's like when you are walking down a street you don't know well, with your girlfriend, near where she lives. The shops are olde fashioned and interesting. You can smell the restaurants. The people on the street are happy and lively. For no reason you look up. In between the buildings you see a piece of the sky, crisscrossed by telephone wires. And you think, the sky looks great. But then you think, not really conscious of it, that the sky is not very important unless you are in a plane or something. But you had a fleeting feeling, just for half a second, that there must be something vast somewhere out there. Something magnificent, someplace where there are heroes and spectacular vistas and things to do beyond what you can imagine or even dream. The vision vanishes quickly. You bring yourself back to reality. You catch each other's eye, the whole world drenched in dopamine and delight, and you feel ten feet tall. You think about what you will order and impending bliss, and talk about whatever, and you are happy.

We do not all have the tools to crack the code of reality. We may not even know there are tools. Or that there is a code to crack. But there is.

Here is an interesting poem. It is interesting partly because it sounds so good in Japanese. Like the sound of a stream as you step over it. And also because a cascade of feeling and ideas flow so freely from it:

この道や

行く人なしに

秋のくれ

Pronounced:

Kono michi ya

Yuku hito nashi ni

Aki no kure

Sometimes translated:

Along this country road

Goes no one

This autumn evening

That first line could also be "This road, and⋯" Meaning "here is a path, and⋯"

The second can be read "goes no one" or "no one goes." The first way is sometimes interpreted as pointing to the no-self nature of the poet walking along, or his complete union with the natural world he inhabits, the Taoist ideal, as he harmonizes with it and is indistinguishable from it.

But this line can also be taken in the sense that – "here is a path and no one is taking it⋯" The word pronounced "Michi" is also pronounced "Dō ," literally meaning a path or way or road. It also a cognate of Tao, understood to mean the way of all things, or the way things are, or a path of personal cultivation. As is "karate-dō ."

There is no "this" in the Japanese in the third line. It just says: "Autumn's evening" or it could be "Autumn's ending."

This path, and no one on it, Autumn is ending

or

This path, No one is going, Absorbed in Autumn

The constellation of images is rich. When a cascade of allusion floods the mind there is no reason to pick one. No matter which way you hear it, the sense of impermanence, the passing of time and moving through space, is clear.

The contemplation of impermanence is the classic entry point to vipassana or insight practice. This practice is most acute when your mind is clear and stable, in samadhi, which allows for sustained, focused attention.

Observation of impermanence begins by noting the arising and passing away of phenomena. The breath is used as the object of attention on which this observation is made, because it is easily accessible and always available. But there are many other objects which are recommended, such as the arising and passing away of feelings, or the changing postures of the body. There are many ways to observe this rise and fall of phenomena which characterize impermanence.

This recognition gives access to observing the other two characteristics of all phenomena. Until we train to recognize them, we miss them, and this deficient view traps us and holds us back from freedom.

As we get used to noticing the impermanence of phenomena, we begin to note the unsatisfactory quality of objects and states of mind. This unsatisfactory quality is the second of the three characteristics of all phenomena. This isn't hard to understand, or horrible when you see it. It means that we are never really finished, never fully satisfied, there is always something uncomfortable or painful. Something more to be done. This does not seem like the biggest deal, at first. But after a while it becomes burdensome and then ominous. When will the wanting end? When will the danger be over? When will we have peace?

As we know, Mick Jagger couldn't get no satisfaction. If he, in the incandescent moments of his ascent, couldn't find satisfaction, we may conclude that, by conventional means at least, satisfaction can't be gotten. Even if he was not speaking for himself alone, but giving voice to the feelings of his millions and millions of fans, which he surely was, which is why he sold all those millions of recordings, we can reach the same conclusion.

That is why we want to recognize unsatisfactoriness, deeply and clearly. So, we can figure out how to do away with, and get some peace, finally.

If the Mick Jagger reference seems antique or obscure: The song it refers to was written in 1964. The Japanese poem above is from 1694. The poet who wrote the poem was called Basho. He lived at the time when Japan was closed off from the rest of the world. Both the poem and the song point to a world of experience familiar to us here and now. The song is a good complement to a Zen poem, which deftly and elegantly evokes impermanence, because no genre screams impermanence like love songs. They come in three flavors: yearning, rapture and nostalgia. That's it. You can follow the lieder back centuries before the birth of rock n' roll, and find the same pattern. The pattern continues in every genre.

The third of the three characteristics of phenomena is that none have a permanent essence, sometimes expressed as no-self-nature. This is a recognition that all phenomena which arise will pass away, that all phenomena are based on causes and conditions, which change, and as they change, the phenomena they have produced change too.

This insight, even the suggestion of it, can feel unsettling and disorienting. Why would you even want to see the world this way?

Partly because it is that way. And because without seeing this we are trapped. What is so profound and liberating about this, what makes this something other than sophistry or speculation, is that it shows how, by engaging in wholesome action we can produce joy and freedom, and have the results we want. We are not stuck in a fixed constellation of unsatisfactory conditions, or in a permanent, suffering life. That's why. This awareness does not lead to extinction, nihilism, or carelessness. It leads to freedom from suffering; the freedom to do some good for the world.

That is what this poem points to. In every line. We usually note the arising of phenomena, we note the things we like and the things we don't like as they appear. Noting the arising and passing away is an intermediate step. Noting the continual passing away of phenomena is next. The poem does this. This has direct implications for effective martial arts practice as a practical matter and as a liberative technique.

***

Part Three
Form

型 Kata

The Japanese character for the word "kata" shows two hands linked together using an implement to cut into the earth.

To build a house you pour a foundation. Before you pour the concrete, you dig into the earth. You build a form, out of wood, that will hold and shape the concrete. You pour the concrete into the form. You give it time. Once the concrete cures it will make a strong, stable foundation for the house. Once the concrete cures you can remove the form.

In Japanese the wooden form is called a kata.

Concrete continues to increase in strength for many years. People who use kata for training also increase in strength for many years. The simile holds in other ways:

A well-made form will serve its purpose. A poorly made one will not. The soundness of the finished work will depend both on the quality of the form and on the quality of the material which fills it.

As traditional practitioners we use kata to perfect our combative skills and to refine our bodies and minds. We pour ourselves into the kata every day. Not once, but again and again.

It is not a matter of becoming rigid and fixed like concrete, or becoming a robot or a machine, repeating the same thing over and over. By pouring ourselves into the kata fresh, every day, we refine our skills and transform our lives. We enter the kata in an immediate way, with the living material of our bodies and minds. By entering the form, by trying to fulfill the ideal of the form, we change. The same kata produces more complete results as time goes by.

The metal used to craft a fine sword blade is smelted from ore. Once it has been refined and prepared, it is melted and poured into a mold. The mold shapes the metal. In Japanese that mold is also called a "kata."

Shaping the metal in the mold is one step in a long process. Heating and cooling, adding layers of material, removing impurities and imperfections, grinding and polishing are precise steps on the path, as the form and substance of the blade are perfected.

No matter how good the quality of the metal, if the form was flawed, the process will fail. The strength, sharpness and resilience of the finished blade depends on the kata in which it first took shape.

As a "template, a style, a pattern, a mold, a form, a posture, or a standard procedure" we have a practical sense of how the word "kata" is used and understood.

But in the words of the 13th century Zen monk Dogen's " "Genjokoan" - Actualizing the Present Moment" - we have a transcendent one. Maybe it is possible for karateka to practice genjo kata – fully alive in a fully living universe, where we are, as we move, every moment, every day, for as long as we practice, for as long as we live.

Chojun Miyagi's motto **"Oku myo zai ren shin"** – **"Deeply hidden reality arises in training the heart and mind"** – is at once a practical and transcendent presentation of the idea. It is at once a command for action and a template for contemplation.

The relationship between form and content, between change and continuity, between life and our tools, between pattern and spontaneity – the reconciliation of all these apparent dichotomies – challenges the way we think and live. Its penetration is essential work for sincere practitioners.

Empress Wu ruled China in the 7th century. She was not able to grasp this. She needed to. Fazang, her imperial advisor, a master of the Hua-yen school used the metaphor of a statue of a golden lion to make it clear. Gold is poured into a form. There it takes on the form of a lion. We see the statue. We recognize a lion. The gold was gold before it was a lion. It will be gold when the statue of the lion is melted. Forms are real, but they are temporary. Something continues – gold in this example – and takes on new form, as conditions change. That is what we do.

We use kata to prepare for combat. We use kata to get strong, fast, resilient, determined, patient, peaceful and fierce. Understand: If you only work kata in your training it is like only building the forms for the foundation of a building. We need great forms. But we can't stop there. We need to fill the kata with life, and then to build on it – with our spirit, purpose and mastery.

That way we continue to construct our style, our skills, and our lives.

***

A Different Ken Zen 拳禅

Empress Wu understood. For us, recognizing apparent contradictions as polarities is also essential.

The expression Ken Zen Ichi Nyo – 拳禅一如 – Fist and Zen as One – was derived from Ken Zen Ichi Nyo – Sword and Zen as One 剣禅一如.

The Sword version was used by Zen priest Takuan Soho (1573-1645) when he was teaching the officials of the Japanese samurai government. The Fist version was adopted by Shoshin Nagamine (1907-1997) as his motto.

This new adaptation of the old yojijukugo, four-character idiom, can be interpreted in several ways. It may be that a profound way of understanding it has not been widely shared.

Karate was imported from Okinawa to Japan in the 1920's. Karate was interpreted in Japan as a kind of empty-hand kendo. Kendo was the elite martial art. It was recognized for centuries as the consummate budo: the well-marked path to the complete fusion of mind and body, of tactics and practice, with transcendent potential.

It was natural for Japanese early adopters of karate, a hundred years ago, to transfer these values and ideology to karate. Some technical and tactical ideas were shared too. These innovations eventually influenced karate on Okinawa too.

Although this made karate more accessible and comprehensible, some things were lost in the transition. The fact that karate is to a great degree an anti-grappling art was de-emphasized, with a new emphasis on the first seconds of an exchange – as in kendo. That is a choice with good self-defense rationale, but it does not cover the full range of engagements karate addresses, or the same initial hands-on contact that many of the kata defend against.

The change had its merits, but eventually there was a trade-off: the understanding of the movement encoded in the kata, the meaning of the techniques, the understanding of the body's powers and vulnerabilities, and access to some of the dynamics of practical empty-hand combatives, faded. Although practicing with empty hands, the mutability of postures and technical scope of hands deployed at close range was replaced by a combative approach, like the approach suited to the use of a long, edged weapon, or in the case of empty hands, a quick exchange resolved by blunt force. This is evident in today's karate kumite matches.

The full range of practical application of karate cannot be realized with that modification. Still, we should not overlook the wisdom we are being offered. The implications of Ken Zen Ichi Nyo, "Fist and Zen as One", are profound – and inspiring – in an unexpected way.

A fist 拳 is not the same as a hand 手 ("hand" is the character "te" in kara te 空手.)

A fist is closed. It does not grasp. It does not cling. It is free to move. It can penetrate and withdraw, deflect and dart, rise and fall. This observation is a pointer, it is a metaphor we can put into practice.

The character Zen 禅 in this four-character motto might refer to the religious movement imported to Japan from China in the 12th century; it might refer to the Zen institution that flourished in Japan the centuries that followed; but there is more to 禅 than the Zen school.

"Zen" as mentioned, is the Japanese pronunciation of the Indian word JHANA (in Pali), DHYANA (in Sanskrit). Dhyana refers to a state of deep concentration and clarity. Through the cultivation of dhyana, we can use the power of our mind to scrutinize experience, to examine phenomena, and to act – with superhuman acuity. Dhyana, Zen in this broader sense, is the foundational skill which makes liberative insight possible.

Then "拳禅一如" can mean "non-clinging – freedom of action – and dhyana – profound clarity – are to be practiced as one." This is why some feel such a close affinity to this motto. It is represented on the calligraphy Sakiyama Sogen gave to me. It is the motto appearing behind Nagamine Shoshin, in his zazen portrait. The vision of the transcendent potential of martial arts was elevated in the karate world through the cultural exchange between Okinawa and Japan a century ago.

This insight, and its implication in practice, are available to all of us. Regardless of style or art, each of us has a chance to realize its truth.

Ken Zen Ichi Nyo, brushed by Sakiyama Sogen

Nagamine Shoshin with Ken Zen Ichi Nyo
drawing by Tarleton Brooks

***

Renzoku 連続

"Renzoku" as it is used in our training does not mean "no count," and it does not mean slow motion. It means "continuous." Renzoku practice is complementary to, but distinct from, the practice method that emphasizes the explode-and-release cycle for each individual technique. In the Flow chapters earlier, the word Zanshin was used to describe the "continuing mind" aspect of the flow state – a state of awareness that flows on uninterrupted even as conditions change. Renzoku is a complementary term, describing the continuity of physical movement during flow.

In "explode and release" practice we isolate each move, and emphasize the compression and release phases of each technique. We learn to increase compression – using all the muscles of the body to, for example, move the elbows to the center line, raise the knee to the chest, make full use of the waist rotation, create vertical or concave shoulder and hip compression, while we enter or evade, gaining advantageous range for follow up, and simultaneously establishing a secure foundation.

In explode and release training we also increase the expansion phase of each move, using full extension of the body weapons – the arms, legs, hands, feet, elbows, knees, etc. – to and through the target, while using full extension of the spine arch, and full use of the helical waveform of energy produced at the waist, as it moves through the body, down to the root and out to the target.

This way we learn to draw the opponent in, maneuver, and generate power with full commitment, maximum energy transfer to the target, and optimal, full-body integration, on every move.

Isolating each move and learning how to optimize it is necessary and valuable. As a result of this we are able to increase the amplitude of the compression-release cycle – getting quick, complete compression and fast, full expansion without resistance in the opposing muscles of each limb.

And we also get the ability to increase the frequency at which we can produce the cycle: for rapid fire, rapid follow-up, powerful techniques. But leaving it at that omits a key dimension of renzoku training which is an indispensable next step for mastery.

Renzoku can be done vigorously or slowly. Either way, it gives an opportunity to explore two other critical aspects of how we move.

One, we examine the interconnections or "arch structures" within the body, required to optimize each move. We learn how to move all the components of our body in relation to one another, creating a single structure – and then how to optimize the transitions, as we shift from move to move.

Two, we examine our performance of the move. If there are flaws in our balance, if there is a place where there is a weight shift, a cant off-axis, or some adjustment or compensation that occurs after the move is done – any sign of imbalance or displacement – we will detect it more easily when moving in slow motion, fluid renzoku.

We can feel what is happening at a more subtle level when moving through the kata. Moving fast is essential for combative skill. But in training, when moving fast, it is possible to overlook some balance issues which do not appear significant when we are practicing on our own. But in contact with an opponent these flaws in posture, flow and balance can create unforced errors, and open gaps which can be exploited by an opponent. This is why we need to build the habit of full commitment to each move. And then we need to build on that skill: to train the posture transformations as we flow from move to move.

In renzoku we connect with the action of the opponent. We can do this with clear understanding of the bunkai in our mind's eye, or in contact with a training partner. This is indispensable for high skill kata training and for effective combatives.

If we simply reposition our body in space, even if the postures are sound and all the elements of form are polished, the connection between the waist, ground, body-weapon and target will be incomplete.

By having a muscle-memory understanding of the bunkai for each movement we will gradually unify our body, because our intention for each technique, and our opponent's intention, will be clear. Then, our energy will follow a complete pathway, making a firm connection between the waist, hara, foundation, and the contact point at the target – thus unifying our body, tactics and will in a single, purposeful combative motion.

Renzoku, continuous flow practice, is a key element of kata training for skill mastery, body and mind unification, and for self-defense application.

It is applied to both contact and kata training.

***

Which Yields Balance in Space, Time and Mind

Perfect balance is dynamic – changing as conditions change. This is a fundamental skill.

Balance in Space

You notice that you are overextended toward your target. Arm outstretched in a punch, maybe you feel too much weight on your front foot, you notice your spine axis is projecting over your front foot, too close to the tipping point.

You sense the vulnerability in this and correct it, bringing the balance back to the vertical centerline, so you are at once stable and mobile, reducing the chance that your opponent will be able to take you off balance. You may notice you are leaning back, or to the side, or crouching as you move. You use proprioception, your internal body awareness, to detect the flaw and fix it, training the habits of balance in space.

Balance in Time

You may notice that you are anticipating or hesitating.

You are off balance in time. Maybe your opponent sets up an expectation, feints or weaves, and then changes his rhythm tricking you into launching an attack, milliseconds too early.

Or let's say you move before the count during group practice, leaning forward in time, anticipating the count instead of responding to it, you can detect the habit of anticipation, and fix it.

If your opponent drops his guard, stumbles, or allows a gap when he fails to land a technique, hesitation will prevent you from countering spontaneously, putting you, however briefly, at a disadvantage. During training we learn to remain in the present, that is, we stay centered in time.

Balance in Mind

During training your mind may drift to what happened before. You may regret an error, or think of something you should have done earlier in the day.

This is leaning back in time. This habit of mind pulls you out of the present, distracts you and puts you off balance. Your attention may be drawn to a person across the room or a sound across the street.

Pulling your mind far from the center, just for an instant. Thoughts about the future, about a plan of attack, an opportunity you want, about tomorrow's demands, or of your next technique, may intrude into your mind in the heat of the moment – in practice or in confrontation. This leaning forward in time also leaves you off balance – not centered here and now, where you can be stable or mobile, where you can choose what to do.

This leaning of the mind can be disastrous. It will create flaws in performance and dangers in combatives which will appear as imbalance in space and time, but are sourced from imbalances in mind.

Our physical and mental habits inform each other. We can analyze them as if they were separate but they are not separate in function.

By learning to maintain centered balance in space, time and mind, as we notice imbalances and fix them – our skills improve in all three dimensions.

Balance Under Threat and at Peace

Presence of mind is useful in everything we do. It is not esoteric. But it needs to be cultivated.

Takuan Soho advised warriors to keep their minds "unfettered", neither stuck nor moving – to intention, target, distraction, or plans. He advised them to keep their minds free of proliferation of thought, free from expectations based on habit – to keep their will unbound. This condition will allow them to perceive instantly and to respond spontaneously in the chaotic dynamics of confrontation.

This is fundamental to the training that we do every day. After a while, we can use this mind training to go deeper.

We develop stability around the center line – dynamic and static – in space, time and mind as we train. But the closer we examine it, the more evident it is that there is no "center line." It does not exist as a thing. It exists in relation to everything around it.

It exists relative to everything around it. The rotation of a wheel works this way. You can see the hub. You can see the axel. You can direct your attention closer and closer to the center of the axel. If you take a microscopic look at the axel, you will see that the atoms themselves are rotating around an axis. If there is one single atom at the middle, it is rotating too. Go in deeper. Maybe you can see the quarks and bosons moving around, but there is no thing, no structure, that is the center. The center is relative and changing. In practice we master this characteristic of our own center line.

Even in static poses, as in the naihanchi kata, the center functions in this way.

The center of the body, as we "draw the four points into the barrel," as we absorb the pressure of shimēi – body pressure and impact training, as we proceed from the initiation of a static posture, through its duration, to its conclusion and its transformation into the next static posture, maintaining the center is essential.

We use it, we rely on it for stability and power. But it is a reference point, not a thing. The center is moving in space and time. It is relative and transitory.

Once we see the relative and changing nature of phenomena, we practice to deepen and sustain that insight, instead of ignoring it or taking it as external to our concerns.

One technique some people use to dial this in is attention on the sensation of the breath at the nostrils, which is mindfulness of breathing. This trains practitioners to reel the attention in, from the years, moments, and instants of the past and from imaginings of the future, to the present.

We can get good at this. Clear and stable, attending to the content of the moment, our body, our feelings, our perceptions, our volitions, our consciousness.

We can do this in meditation to train it, but we can do it anytime in any posture. As we get good at it we use this sharp presence of mind in partner practice, kumite or combatives – when even a millisecond of deviation from awareness in the present moment may get us feedback we don't want.

Even in breath-awareness meditation or in kumite, our attention can never grasp the present moment. We get close. But we can never get hold of it.

The present-ness of the present moment is not apprehensible, it is not graspable, it is not observable. The present is a reference point, not a thing. It is relative, like the center line of the body or the center point of a wheel.

And the closer we look for it, no matter now acute the attention or how small the frame of reference, it continues to elude us. It is not a thing. It is an infinitely remote reference point. At human scale, at ordinary ranges of performance, that is not critical. But to overlook this fact is an obstacle, if you are seeking to break through to the truth, put an end to confusion, and be free.

We cannot comprehend infinities. We can describe them and frame them.

But the conventional ways of imagining and depicting infinity – as a moving star field like in a movie about outer space, or a vanishing point perspective moving toward the horizon, a graph or a mathematical formula – are necessarily metaphoric or approximate or both.

We can gain direct experience of the present through training.

There are many techniques used to deepen our ability to experience time and space at finer and finer scales. When we do deeper observation of the moment we are in, or the changes in the postures as we pass through them, the experience is something like looking at a fractal zoom. There is no end to it. We pass a reference point as we move in for a closer look. We are disconcerted briefly then we can reorient in the new fractal landscape, at the new dimension.

That detachment from scale is not an objective in itself, but a training tool. It dissolves our presumption that our human-scale perspective is the only real and only relevant one. It increases our sense of magnitude and our access to magnificence.

It enables us to escape the confines of our own self-regard, the limits of our vanities, blunders and burdens. It allows us to enter the presence of the infinity of life and possibility, hidden by our habits of mind, which we took as definitive and real, but now we can see, were artificial. So, it's a handy, practical tool. Even those of us who got into karate for completely different reasons.

The same surprising reorientation in scale occurs as you are reading the Gandhavyuha – the Entry into the Realm of Reality, referenced by Takuan, with its narration of traveling through the 52 stages of training to enlightenment – or the Vimalakirtinirdesa Sutra, among the most popular sutras in Chinese Buddhism. This change-of-scale technique is used in many ancient texts in this genre.

These books describe universes as existing in every pore of a being's skin, galactic world systems poised on every hair. A desperate days-long race across the world to escape the wrath of an angry god, arriving relieved and exhausted, only then discovering that the poor creature running all that time has been running across the palm of the hand of the serene titan he was sure he could evade.

They describe phantasmagorical settings where millions of beings flock from other worlds, galaxies and universes to meet in a man's home, and once there, in his little room, find thrones for each one of them thousands of miles high, and find plenty of room for all the thrones and for everyone to sit, without being crowded, without changing the room at all.

These are stories, not depositions. They are entertaining, but that is not why they have been told.

As we read, it is as if we have entered an infinite hall of mirrors, we see the endless interpenetration of scales replicated, from the cosmic to the infinitesimal. We notice variations as we travel through them, while somehow the new worlds remain familiar. As we go, it becomes easier and more natural to reorient, to understand, and to experience the new world, and still know what we are up to.

This is a training tool. Like learning new kata, a task which itself gets easier as you go. It gets easier as you become accustomed to the experience of going from not knowing what you are doing to familiarization to mastery. We reorient more easily as new information comes our way. We recognize patterns more quickly. Things make more sense.

In the case of the ancient texts, the excursion is a literary one; it is imaginary. In the case of the fractal zoom our visual adventure takes place in a graphic representation of a mathematical idea. They are imaginary but they can illuminate something quite real in our experience. The shifts in perspectives matter because with a rigid, self-centered world view our minds become rigid, and our knowledge remains limited. Our actions, based on old, limited information, deviate more and more from the way things are. We fail to get the results we want.

Understanding experience from multiple perspectives is essential for any leader, any fighter, any person. To be effective a leader has to understand the viewpoints of his peers, his competitors, the people working for him, the people he is working for, his customers, clients, suppliers and many others. That leader needs to know that those perspectives may be different from his and may be valid. They comprise the operational environment. He will need to understand their views if he is to persuade them of his. And if he is to learn from them. Leaders do this in all time frames – seconds from now, in days, quarters, years, decades. For a leader, and for all of us, all those scales matter. There are times when it is wise to consider scales much greater, and much smaller than what we usually see.

The bug on your hand who would prefer not to die, just like you. The important person with nuclear bombs who would see things differently if he could see from the point of view of the billions of people who will have to die to make the omelet.

Or how many objects, colors, patterns and details we pick up and miss as we scan a room or a face. How many components are involved when the arm moves, the body turns, the eyes grasp the potential.

How much can you accelerate your ability to observe, orient, decide and act, or to understand. How far can you step back to observe the contours of a lifetime, a family, a culture, a history, a world. How much better could we perform if we could shift perspectives quickly, or hold them all at once. How much more could we do for people?

We saw the world differently ten years ago than we do now. Maybe we had strong opinions then. Maybe we have different strong opinions now. We will see the world differently in the future. It is useful to note this and to continue to learn, continue to be humble, bold and ceaseless in our effort to do right.

Our quest for the present, here and now, as we practice, as we carefully observe phenomena as they change, as they transform from moment to moment, based on their composition and their conditions, gradually gives us the ability to see deeply, and to become free of the confusion and pain that comes from our attachment to our limited and distorted impressions of things, as they are and as they change.

Insight, into the present moment in time, into the center of our bodies in space – as we move, stand, walk, sit or lie down, is also a mind excursion. That excursion - like the fractal zoom, like the profusion of beings and universes in the ancient books, like advanced kata practice and careful attention – are paths that we can take to understanding, then to insight and then to freedom.

To be able to prevent a violent attack is a valuable skill. To subdue a violent threat to takes courage and training. It is worth all the spirit and effort we devote to it. It is an obligation and an honor to do what we can. We build those skills.

Over a lifetime, we build on them.

***

Stable Equilibrium

As we train, without noticing it, we live in an increasingly stable equilibrium. That does not happen automatically. But if you practice well it will happen. It is essential for every able person, martial artist or not.

A stable equilibrium system tends to return to stability when it is disturbed. Imagine a ball at the bottom of a bowl. It will sit there. Until you give it a push. Then it will roll around. How much it rolls depends on how hard you push, the weight of the ball, and the shape of the bowl. But within the limits of the system, the ball will eventually settle down and return to a stable position at the center of the bottom of the bowl. That is a stable equilibrium.

An unstable equilibrium initially may appear to be stable. Stand a nail on its head at the bottom of the bowl. It is at equilibrium. Then give it a push. It tips over. It will not stand back up. It just lays there. You could say it has found a new equilibrium, its potential energy exhausted, fallen over, and not able to recover. It does not return to its initial equilibrium point, like the ball did.

A stable equilibrium system is resilient. It can absorb shock, gain energy, retain its system integrity, recover, and be ready to go again.

We are subject to disturbances continually. Some we notice. Most we do not. Trauma and life changes are stressors we notice. What generally flies under the radar is the torrent of feelings and perceptions which attract us, repel us, seduce us, threaten us and bore us, nonstop, all day. They all produce movement in our heart and mind, and we hardly notice.

Someone we pass on the street who looks menacing. Someone who looks beautiful. Some people we experience as obstacles in our path. We may spot someone interesting, someone we will never know. And on and on. The pictures in the windows, the look of the pavement, the shape of the horizon, a plant, a lot, a coffee cup, a landscape, a sign, a building façade, a scent of cooking and of pigeons, a gust of wind, a leaf, a pile of trash, a flock of birds, a dog – all of it, a thousand times a second, impinging on our senses, leaving its trace, submerged, unremarked in the flood of impressions. The news, movies, songs, dialogues, the sights and sounds devised and directed at us, we consume without paying much attention, as if they were merely external, merely the environment, as if they were out there at a distance while we are in here, safe in the harbor of our own mind. But they do influence us. So much so that they begin to constitute our world, form our values, guide our ideas and thinking, and impel our actions. And we never knew what hit us.

It is difficult to navigate in that fog. But we can. We can see it, and see through it. And we can make the fog disappear. You might not think martial arts could help to do this. But it can.

Everyone knows water will adapt to the shape of its container. Pour it into a cylinder, a cup, an ocean, a drain, the water just adapts and flows and goes with it. No questions asked.

Animals adapt to their environment. When animal populations grow, some move to a new area. When water is scarce, they stay as close as they dare to the spring. When predators get hungry, they range wider. When predators are on the move, prey move to their holes, their trees, their nests.

People adapt too. But unlike water or animals – we can modify our environment by choice and by will, and we can choose how we adapt to it. When our environment is pathological, we may adapt in a pathological way. If people are deprived of access to the transcendent, we may learn to behave like animals – running from pain, scurrying toward pleasure. Preoccupation with food, sex, intoxication, money and status stand in for a purposeful life.

Sitting in traffic, doing meaningless, stifling work, sitting and watching strangers pretend to do things they aren't doing in recorded performances, on TV and in movies, our attention and our hearts are pulled toward expressions of dissatisfaction and desire depicted in these media which seem to mirror and confirm what we feel. We respond this way to pop culture, news, ads and entertainment, without questioning the mental environment that is being made for us to live in. Without realizing that it is substituting for taking hold of our own life, for doing things worth doing, like venturing out, on our own or with others, toward freedom.

But to do that you have to know that such a thing is possible. Then you have to learn how it might be done. Then can you do it. Martial arts has the potential to provide a stable platform on which we can do this work. Here are some of the ways we can use it:

-Taking control of your priorities, your time and your schedule.

-Using your time purposefully – moment to moment, in pursuit of your goal.

-Getting your body healthy, flexible and strong, so you feel good and confident.

-Getting your will strong so that you can stand up for yourself easily and naturally, without resorting to aggression when it is not called for, and having access to it if it is.

-Developing positive, respectful relationships: Appreciating seniors for their skill, and for their help. Taking an interest in the development of newer people. Helping them along, recognizing that their success is as important as yours, because it is a part of yours, and that to them it is more important. Guiding people from the start, with respect, when they are taking their first tentative steps. Challenging and collaborating with your peers, even when the competition gets heated.

-Developing intense, sustained focus: Little by little, with attention and repeated effort, we can maintain sharp attention on exactly what we are doing – at first for a few seconds at a time, then for one kata, for a few minutes, then for the duration of the training session, even one that goes on for hours.

-Entering into advanced flow states in which our body, mind and will are fused in skillful present-time action, without conscious thought. These states are familiar to high performers in every field. They are accessible to every one of us.

Based on these aspects of dojo training it is possible to go deeper. Doing deep mind training, moving and seated, develops a highly refined sensitivity of mind that can detect the influences we are subject to, and our subtle, fleeting responses to them, as they happen; influences which may be toxic and destabilizing, which we need to recognize, understand, guard against or abandon. At the same time we detect influences which are nourishing and can be cultivated.

Using this heightened awareness we can replace the pathological influences, and the states of body and mind that result from them, with healthy states of body and mind. Based on the momentum formed from our habit of training consistently and sincerely, we can deepen and extend these capacities to unimagined depth.

In this way we develop stable equilibrium as the condition of life. We will encounter turbulence, disturbances, even direct threats. We are not immune. But we are not easily off-balanced. When we are disturbed, we can recover and respond to the demands of the situation – combative or otherwise – skilfully, without hesitation or haste.

Through good training we extend the range of our life. The same hand can caress a face, play a concerto, cut a tree, break a brick and sweep the dojo clean. We need to be able to respond to conditions based on what is right and good: to take action based on what will further our aspirations and benefit the people who depend on us.

Exaggerating the possibilities of martial arts training – claiming budo magically sets your feet on the path to enlightenment – obscures the depth of what is actually available, and prevents people from making the most of their training.

***

手, The Lost Art of the Frozen Hunter

By exploring our kata we discover tactics and develop skills we can use inside and outside the dojo. These insights are not evident when looking at the movement of the kata from the outside.

They appear when you are inside the kata, doing it, with training partner-opponents, while investigating the movement, the intention, and the effects of each action.

Exciting work is being done around the world on the bunkai, analysis, of Okinawan karate kata. But still, some of the legacy bunkai has been frozen to death. Watching it is a little like coming upon the body of an ancient hunter, frozen in the ice in a mountain cave ages ago, bow and arrows still in his hands. You can see from his skin and bones, his equipment and his face, evidence of the kind of life he lived. And you can see he is not living it anymore.

He might have a lot to teach us if we could bring him back to life. We can't do that, and we can't bring back the men who knew this material, but we can revive the kata bunkai, and with it, kata practice and fighting skill.

The revival is happening because we are using knowledge of combatives drawn from experience and from a broad spectrum of fighting skills, with patience, persistence, experimentation, examination and application testing under pressure.

On Okinawa, the indigenous martial art was called te, 手, hands. It was not called 拳法, ken-po. Ken-po is translated as "fist art" or literally "fist law". But either way, that first character is fist. Not hands.

Karate is an anti-grappling art. Of course, we learn to strike – with hands and feet, elbows and knees and other parts of the body – to stop a threat. But much of what we are learning to do is to defeat a grappling attack.

People grapple because that's what they learned to do – by learning wrestling and other grappling and throwing arts, or by watching them. It is a natural instinct - we grab and hold on. People learn martial arts like boxing, Japanese karate, Muay Thai, Tae Kwon Do, kick boxing and other striking arts too. But refereed matches aside, no matter what they learned, in a violent encounter, as fighters lose energy, after 20 seconds or maybe a minute of furious full-power punching and kicking, they begin to clinch, hold on, try to restrain their opponent's blows or pin their opponent down.

Takedowns are not our go-to solution. There are only three takedowns where we go to the floor in all the moves of the 18 kata we practice. One in Wanshu (the same one as in Pinan Godan), and one in Chinto.

We rely on throwing, and of countering attempted throws. These are used repeatedly in every kata. Their use is distinct from the give and take familiar in matches in throwing-based arts. We are not aiming for a pin or attempting to roll out and re-engage. We are intending to end the threat, with a dislocation or impact, and follow up if necessary.

For a detailed explanation of how we use these concepts see Appendix Two.

***

Naihanchi's Strange Omission

In learning "te", the indigenous Okinawa fighting art which evolved into karate, some practiced only naihanchi kata for the first three years.

Naihanchi does not present a full spectrum fighting system. Motobu Choki, a leading Okinawan teacher of Shorin Ryu from the early 20th century, said it was all you needed for proficiency as a fighter.

Photos of his kumite and drills show that he does not limit his movement to the naihanchi kata techniques. He turns in all directions and uses many postures and techniques which do not appear in the naihanchi kata. He relied on grabbing and throwing, as well as striking. Motobu uses naihanchi as his fundamental training method, but not as his only source of technique. He was known to be massive and powerful. Naihanchi suited him.

There are no high defensive techniques in naihanchi. This may point to its purpose: that Naihanchi is designed to train practitioners in the "earth element" aspect of the body and mind.

The attributes of the earth element are solidity and substance. The earth element is stable, massive, inert and hard to dislodge.

Funakoshi Gichin, prominent Okinawan teacher of Shorin Ryu karate in Japan in the early 20th century, called these kata Tekki – iron horse kata. Funakoshi and Motobu did not see eye to eye.

But they both emphasized the fundamental importance of naihanchi training.

The reason we train with this kata thoroughly is that the earth element, which is strong and stable, provides the proper foundation for the construction of strong, stable karate, just as the earth element provides the proper foundation for the construction of a strong, stable building.

When you put up a building you make sure the earth beneath it is stable, and that there is no water moving there. You make sure there are no voids, air pockets that would weaken the structure. You make sure there is no wood present – no stumps, roots or buried branches which could decompose or burn.

This is analogous, using Chinese five elements theory, to the use of naihanchi in constructing the training foundation of a karate-ka. Three years of naihanchi makes a powerful foundation on which to build a lifetime of training.

To defend against attacks to the head and neck, whether strikes, chokes or seizing, it is best to use rising and dropping and turning, as we do in all our other kata. High strikes, associated with fire element, are not well-defended with earth element postures or techniques. We have many other tools in our kit to use in response to attacks to the head. Of course, there are many techniques in the naihanchi kata that can be interpreted as striking or seizing the head of your opponent. But these are used when he is bent, and his head is low.

The unexpected front-to-back stability of the stance substantiates the earth-element interpretation of naihanchi. Although the side-to-side stability of the stance is well-recognized and easy to master, the front to back stability is sometimes overlooked and difficult to master. Sometimes people do not know how to establish the naihanchi posture so that it is powerfully rooted front-to-back when put under pressure, and so miss bunkai applications that make use of this aspect of the posture. (*This is described in Appendix Two.*)

***

正念 Mindfulness in Kata

At the same time that my technical exploration was underway I was also seeking a classically-derived, currently-used, real, reliable, wholesome approach to mind training which enables technical mastery and liberation, using martial arts. Which is a lot to ask. But I am hardly the first to seek it. Some solutions have been developed which have not been applied to martial arts.

We practice mindfulness of the body from the day we begin karate training. Our physical skills, sharp awareness and practical self-defense ability are built on the interpenetration and fusion of the body and mind.

The Greatest Warrior

They say that the greatest warrior masters himself. This mastery might refer to impulse control – i.e., achieving the freedom of mind and skill in technique to take appropriate action at the decisive moment, with no hesitation and no haste. To some people self-mastery means the cultivation of a clear, present-focused mind, stable in the midst of the chaos of combat and the seductions of peace.

These have been central concerns of great practitioner-theorists from Musashi Miyamoto to John Boyd.

They are lofty goals, difficult to achieve. But they are limited goals. There is more to self-mastery than this.

The problem:

···"It might be assumed that we are always aware of the present, but this is a mirage. Only seldom do we become aware of the present in the precise way required by the practice of mindfulness. In ordinary consciousness the mind begins a cognitive process with some impression given in the present, but it does not stay with it. Instead, it uses the immediate impression as a springboard for building blocks of mental constructs··· The mind perceives its object free from conceptualization only briefly. Then, immediately after grasping the initial impression, it launches on a course of ideation by which it seeks to interpret the object to itself, to make it intelligible in terms of its own categories and assumptions. To bring this about the mind posits concepts, joins the concepts into constructs—sets of mutually corroborative concepts—then weaves the constructs together into complex interpretative schemes. In the end the original direct experience has been overrun by ideation and the presented object appears only dimly through dense layers of ideas and views, like the moon through a layer of clouds.

··· To be sure, the product is not wholly illusion, not sheer fantasy. It takes what is given in immediate experience as its groundwork and raw material, but along with this it includes something else: the embellishments fabricated by the mind···"

The solution is a practical training technique we can use:

"···Mindfulness of the postures focuses full attention on the body in whatever position it assumes··· when changing postures, one is aware of changing postures.

The contemplation of the postures ⋯reveals that the body is ⋯a configuration of living matter subject to the directing influence of volition⋯"
-Bhikkhu Bodhi, <u>The Noble Eightfold Path</u>, p64 and 68, Pariyati Publishing

As we train in mindfulness of the body, we become a unified dynamic system in which body and mind, perception and response, will and action, coalesce.

Training in mindfulness of the body we can extend our present time awareness into every movement, moment and act of will, without interference.

A meditation instruction like "empty the mind" cannot achieve this. A mind simply devoid of content cannot achieve technical mastery or liberation.

Entry to the Realm of Deep Practice

The mindfulness approach has unlimited potential as a gateway to true liberative practice.

The mindfulness approach functions in all dimensions of training. As we train to observe closely, we can detect and remedy deflections of attention which we did not notice or whose significance we did not recognize before. These deflections come as a result either of outward distractions or inner disturbances of the mind. We need not be subject to them.

We can monitor the body more subtly and use it more adeptly.

We can extend the training to all moments of life.

Inner mental disturbances lose their power as our conduct becomes more wholesome – as our actions of body, speech and mind accord with restraint of greed, anger and delusion. As we learn to detect and remedy negative emotions and actions our attention and our will become deeper, sharper and more stable. Our physical skills are released from the constraints of hidden tension, subtle defects in balance, and fragmentation and discontinuity in the motion of the body. You can observe these positive results in high performance athletes, warriors, musicians and others. But it is not possible for an untrained observer to tell how they are achieving their level of self-mastery.

The self-aware, analytic approach is not used during kumite or other high-pressure performance. It is a tool we use as part of the spectrum of training, at the right place and the right time. We don't use calisthenics or do a kata in the heat and pressure of confrontation or kumite either. But they are needed in training to achieve peak performance.

We can use this mind training approach to refine and perfect all the postures of our kata and of all the training we do. We can also make a mental habit of practicing this body-mind awareness outside the dojo setting: when we are walking, standing, sitting and lying down.

Since we always have a posture and we always have a mind we can practice any time.

3D Training in Restraint and Action

The Japanese character for mindfulness, 念, is made of two parts: the one above is "now." The one below is "mind."

With heightened awareness of the condition of our mind we can refrain from unwholesome actions and words before they manifest. As we do, our ability to maintain mindfulness and enter sustained concentration deepens. We can then use that deep attention to examine the more subtle levels of the operation of our body and mind, to cultivate liberating wisdom.

It is this dimension that has been excluded from our tradition, and which is essential for training that is practical here and now and at the same time is aimed at achieving our highest aspirations.

To achieve our goals, we need to conduct a well-informed investigation into the nature of our body and mind as they really are – as changing, seeking, interconnected processes – examining our body, mind and all our experience, for these characteristics. Once we can see these clearly, we can perfect our training, and reach our potential.

***

Mind Training Technique

There are some martial artists who are not satisfied with the Zen approach. Even though they have trained with Zen masters for a long time, worked with martial arts teachers imbued with Zen culture, spirit and training technique, they ask if there isn't something more. Something else.

They wonder if their intuition is supposed to be very acute by now. If sen no sen isn't supposed to be natural for them.

They may imagine that if they need it, it will be there. They feel that, after all this time, they should be able to know their opponent's intention, glimpse the future in a battle, or see around a corner with their minds eye, as described in the books and by their teacher. They wonder if they will be sitting there one day, soon, kneeling on the floor of the dojo at the beginning or end of class, they will start to get "realizations."

For them I will offer this alternative, which has deep roots, is wholesome and nourishing at every step, and rewards effort. This may offer a way to integrate karate kata into a complete path of practice. It is a suggestion for research. This mind training technique, as a complete path of practice is not new. It is well established, widely practiced and elaborately described. Applying this to kata as far as I know is new. I go into some detail here to present the research plan. I present it with the proviso and this is not a do-it-yourself project but requires good guidance from an experienced source.

In some examples I cited earlier – the center point of a wheel, and of the present moment – our words point to things we think we know but whose nature eludes us until we examine them.

Those two exist in relation to their context, but aren't things which can be found, in themselves. In the same way there is no such thing as a footstep, or a breath. Of course, we know what we are talking about when we use those terms, but there is no "thing" that corresponds to the words. Those are processes, transformations. We cannot perceive an essence in them. But we can perceive their arising and passing away, as we can with every posture, every technique, every moment.

This points us to the negations in the Heart Sutra; to kensho, the first glimpse of insight that leads to liberation. This is why attention, focused on just these kinds of changing things, requires intense concentration, and reveals plain truths we ordinarily miss, because we are unable to examine phenomena closely. This is why this direction offers us a solution to the problem of ultimacy – complete spiritual practice – in martial arts training.

In sections of the Satipatthana Sutta, the Anapanasati Sutta, and the Kayagata Sati Sutta as preserved in the Theravada Majjhima Nikaya, training in the establishment of mindfulness begins with mindfulness of breathing. Mindfulness of the postures follows.

In our approach we begin with postures. This is the way presented in the Chinese Madhyama Agama. This version begins with postures as the object of attention, and proceeds to mindfulness of breathing, practiced in a sitting posture.

It is natural for us as karate practitioners to begin with attention on the body. We have been practicing mindfulness of the body from day one in training. Here, in this more advanced approach, we deepen our concentration, mindful of what the body is doing all the time, as a whole, bringing every part and aspect into our awareness.

Establishing mindfulness of the body, according to the tradition, is a direct path to enlightenment. If practiced carefully, as described in the suttas, and interpreted in the commentary and meditation manuals including the Visuddhimagga, it is perfectly suited to lead from mindfulness, to deep concentration, to liberative insight.

I mention the original sources to be clear that this practice is not an innovation. I mention the motives and vision of the practice in the original to make the context of their presentation in the original sources clear.

Using the kata as focus of attention is not a devotional or sectarian practice. A punch, turn, kick or takedown are for everyone. They are not limited to a religious category or purpose. This mind training technique can be practiced this way as well. As a tool to fulfill your objective, within your tradition, your cultures and your values. Many martial arts that have spread around the world were born in east Asia, at a time when Confucianism, Taoism and Buddhism informed the cultural worldview.

Martial arts are now practiced in Japan and China by many people as a modern, secular pursuit. In cultures informed by science, technology, politics, finance, media and the arts.

Martial artists are practicing in Moscow, Warsaw, Berlin, London, Karachi, Jerusalem, Johannesburg, Nairobi, Los Angeles, the bible belt and everywhere else. To a great degree martial artists around the world use the same techniques, get the same skills and the same benefits from training. We live in varied cultures, with varied motives, objectives and beliefs. Tools are tools. People can use them well or poorly, to build or destroy. If we have them, we can use them well, for our purposes. If we don't, we can't. So here we go:

Awareness of postures works naturally for us, as an advanced practice, because by the time we begin this we have already developed a very steady and deep body awareness. It is a natural approach for us because, with a few exceptions, we avoid doing controlled breathing or breath awareness during kata practice.

The mindfulness of the body technique is not something we add on or plug in to our training. It is natural for us to take the body awareness developed in skill training and apply it to concentration and insight training. We can introduce this once the body knowledge is well-developed, the kata are deeply ingrained in muscle memory, and the ability we have cultivated, to concentrate for extended periods on skillful movement, will benefit from more intense concentration and more precise examination and awareness.

This technique simply clarifies how we proceed.

Here is the sequence of the objects of attention that we can use. The first series we use already, as we develop technical skill. Next, we can add sustained attention, with these as the mental objects we are attending to. In the second series we take the next step, building on our sustained, calm attention, to emphasize insight practice.

1.

Components of static posture
Whole body static posture
Static Arches
Dynamic Arches in transition from move to move
Whole body changing from move to move

2.
Arising and passing away of the postures in kata sequence
Passing away of postures in kata sequence
Mindfulness of the whole body, just enough for bare awareness

This sequence is derived from the Satipatthana sutta section on mindfulness of the postures. This material is allusive, conveyed with technical terms which may be unfamiliar. It not fully accessible without study and guidance from experienced people.

This is not a devotional or sectarian practice. It is a mind and body training technique. It works well.
Here is how: the effect of this training can be described with words like tranquility, unification of body and mind, and insight into how things are. Those are not necessarily compelling words.

In the sense that they are used here they do not convey much about the experience or the result of the practice, because when we first encounter this description, the words may not point directly to experiences that we have had, or want. They are theoretical and nice, but, I do not think they are compelling enough to inspire digging into a new and demanding practice.

I will offer this perspective: The experience, as you put effort into this training, as you develop momentum in it, becomes very pleasant. What follows is a feeling of happiness as you practice. Then deep composure which makes the world and all its events and all your experience more comprehensible.

This is not a manufactured, affective state, like what we get through sense experience, when we listen to music or see a movie or have something good to eat. It is experienced within and without.

It is a result of a deepening cognitive consonance. It is the natural result of the dissolving of the cognitive dissonance we all are accustomed to.

This cognitive dissonance is a result of misinterpreting experience, craving what we do not have, holding on to changing things, the anxiety and sadness that accompany framing the world and our experience and our actions based on these habits of mind.

We take that to be the nature of the world and of ourselves, and the natural condition of our lives. But it is not. The disturbance can settle down.

The habit of craving and misunderstanding generates cognitive dissonance, hindrances in the mind, which burden us, as if all our lives we are carrying a heavy weight, as if we are moving through a broken landscape filled with obstacles and unseen dangers, slowing us down and disturbing us as we try to get on with it.

We can eliminate these obstacles. Since they are made of misinterpretation, they have no life of their own. We can live and travel on beautiful land and ascend to the sunlit uplands effortlessly and joyfully.

It does not happen to you just by doing this training. Fighting skill does not happen to you just by doing the training either. You do it. You make it work. You take up the tools and use them again and again until they are your tools, until you can use them well.

Here I only want to suggest how the full three-dimensional potential of our martial arts practice, as proposed for centuries in east Asian martial arts lore – for health, martial skill and the perfection of character – is valid and is available. I believe this synthesis makes it possible to use karate as an integral part of a complete training path.

***

Part Four
War

Bun Bu Ryo Do: Cultivation and Power

Ethics, tactics and metaphysics form a unified field of action. Martial artists who regard them as separate are at a disadvantage. These three dimensions cannot be separated. If you try to separate them, becoming an expert in one and neglecting the others, you may advance temporarily, but you will lose. If you use these as a single system you will have the best chance to prevail and endure.

Bun Bu
brushed by Sakiyama Sogen

Funakoshi's Crisis Intervention

The Karate-Do Kyohan is a concise and comprehensive technical manual. Without confusing beginners, it opens the door to deep understanding for practitioners with the experience to grasp what is there.

In it, Funakoshi Gichin bookends his technical material with personal comments. At the beginning he explains his motive for writing the book: the urgent need to arrest the decline of karate culture, and to preserve it intact for future generations.

At the end of the book, in a brief, two-page note, he lays out the moral and philosophical context for his karate. He draws on the great streams of intellectual and practical knowledge which informed his life and the world into which he was born.

Although he does not call these out, in these two pages he quotes the Mencius – (The Works of Mencius, Book 6, Part 2, Section 15, paragraph 2) one of the "Four Books," the essential educational curriculum for leaders and officials in China for 700 years.

He references the Confucian ideal of the Junzi, with its emphasis on benevolence as the essential human value.

He cites Sun Tzu's famous formula on the critical role of intelligence in marital victory, from the Art of War.

He references the Kenpo Hakku – the Eight Verses on Karate – from the BuBishi, a compilation of karate techniques and ideas, influential in the Okinawan dojo culture of his youth.

He references the subtle skill needed to discern the seeds of coming events – citing the appearance of animals and of sages – again from the Four Books.

He closes with a reminder of the dynamic polarity in which we fight and live, directing his readers' attention to an issue of prime concern in budo, the issue of suki – the gap in defense.

Why does he give this philosophical advice in a book devoted to technique?

These were the texts and ideas which guided him. He learned from them. He used their principles. He wants to share them with his readers and students. He wants to put the technical instruction in the book into context – of action and of meaning. He wants to form an ethical basis for the practice of martial arts, integrated into tactical principles which apply to training and to the proper use of force. He understands that power without virtue leads nowhere.

The traditional mode of writing a persuasive essay, which he used, is to select and organize quotations from authoritative sources and build your argument from there – so there is no question that the author might be "making things up," but rather that he is relying on proven and accepted wisdom to make his case.

Still, it is his experience, wisdom and conviction which inform every word of his brief essay.

He feels the responsibility to include this philosophical conclusion because, whatever our place in the world, we all need guidelines to direct our skill and use our passion wisely.

In his era, as in ours, when passions were inflamed, it was necessary to remind the ardent young men who studied with him, that while the judicious use of force is sometimes necessary, it needs to be matched with a humane respect for individual agency and dignity, in order to have a good effect, and not devolve into darkness and oppression.

His presentation followed a long tradition of leaders, warrior scholars, and cultivated people who sought to balance the principles of Bun 文, matters of civil life, and Bu 武, the conduct of war, in their lives and work.

Bun Bu Ryo Do

For centuries Bun and Bu were the two primary career paths for ambitious young men in China – either in the civil service or the military.

"Bun Bu Ryo Do" was associated with the ideal of the Confucian junzi, "gentleman" or "superior man". In that sphere Bun Bu Ryo Do is sometimes translated as "The way of both pen and sword." Ryo Do means both ways.

The implications are central to statecraft. Following victory in a war of conquest there is a period of consolidation and institution-building, to assure that the conquest will endure, not slip away as the threat of force that holds it together is released. Violence is expensive and destructive. It may succeed in the short term but it is not sustainable.

The scope of Bun includes government, management, literature, science, philosophy, law, religion and scholarship.

Bu is not just skill in arms, or leadership on the battlefield. Bu encompasses the mastery of techniques, tactics, operations, strategy, logistics, technology, planning, mission, morale, communication, intelligence, leadership and more.

The mastery of persuasion and force, and their proper use is a perennial concern. It is an urgent matter for us, now. The 42nd emperor of Japan, who reigned in the 8th century, took the characters for bun and bu, 文武 , as his name. The proper use of Bun and Bu was a key issue in the 12th century Tale of the Genji, the world's first novel, written as the samurai consolidated their power. At the height of the power of the samurai government, warlords recognized the limits of force. Scholar Thomas Conlan notes: **"The 17th century witnessed the resurgence of the bun and bu ideal as a metaphor for governance."**

This is a practical matter for us. Alexander the Great, King Ashoka, Genghis Khan, the American Revolutionaries and their descendants, knew it well. We can see in their examples, that ethics, tactics and metaphysics, function as a unified field of action. We can see it in how they took power and how they ruled and how they vanished from the earth. We can derive insight into the interplay of coercion and persuasion in our own field of action. And we may better understand how the world around us is being created, destroyed, rebuilt and transformed.

Alexander the Great

Alexander the Great's dad was a general, his tutor was Aristotle, and he was a genius in war. Riding over the crest of a hill he could look out over a landscape he'd never seen before and instantly grasp the strategic significance of a bend in a river, the slope of a riverbank, the tactical potential of a slight depression running at the edge of a valley. He could interpret his enemy's order of battle, anticipate their plans, and on the spot form his own.

He overwhelmed much larger armies on their home turf. His soldiers willingly followed him into the unknown, down rivers into unnamed seas, faced world powers and walled cities, and with him they subdued them all.

Alexander did this in campaign after campaign. His brilliant battles, fought in the 4th century BCE, are standard curriculum in War Colleges around the world.

They want to know how he did it. It is also interesting to consider why he did it. The answer is taken for granted, as the modus operandi of the great. But that begs the question. And we would benefit from having an answer. It is also interesting to examine what he did with the vast world he conquered once he got it.

Alexander wanted it all. He was ferocious and calculating, but that's not all he was. They say he was fun to hang out with, a real people person. He conquered the largest empire of his day, Persia, by cunning and force.

But he ruled the empire by embracing Persian cultural forms, keeping their bureaucracy, their bureaucrats, their religion and customs. His conquest was iron and fire. His rule was water and silk.

The subjugated Persians kept their jobs, their homes and their livelihoods. All he wanted was their money and allegiance. He made sure he got that. He installed his best friends in top spots throughout his empire, appointing his leading general Ptolemy as ruler of Egypt. Ptolemy, a Greek, ruled in Egyptian style, assuring that the Greeks remained atop the pyramid of power, and that the lion's share of the wealth and geostrategic benefit accrued to them. No riddle there.

Ptolemy succeeded in holding Egypt for the Macedonians but Alexander's empire dissolved. Alexander's death opened a *suki* that was immediately exploited by his enemies and by his ambitious friends.

Generations of war depleted and fragmented the empire. The areas that now are Greece, Turkey, Afghanistan, Iran, Central Asia, Pakistan, Iraq, Israel, Lebanon, Jordan, India, and beyond – all of which were once "united" by force, into Alexander's empire – went their own ways. Not one of the great warrior generals who conquered together under Alexander's leadership had the skill to rule the empire in time of peace.

The same issues appear in martial arts groups. Charismatic figures appear and disappear. Trends come and they go. Alliances form and dissolve. Organizations need wise leadership, structure, purpose, and reward for merit, or they will lose momentum, become corrupted by ambition or complacency, fragment and vanish.

If we are confronted: Maybe we will stop the assailant in his tracks, or maybe he will run. What if he gets up, energized? What if he comes running back armed? What if we attempt to restrain him, and end up with a thrashing, drug-fueled problem in our hands?

What if we are effective with our initial use of force but not able to maintain control. What about the use of persuasion, to de-escalate and resolve the problem before it goes too far, or to come to terms after the heat of conflict cools?

Bun and Bu matter to us. In our training groups. And in personal defense. This is a small-scale application of the idea, but it is not small when it is your life that depends on getting it right.

Emperor Ashoka

Kings wage war. They expand their frontiers. For millennia that was in the job description.

Like a corporate CEO, an ambitious guy who owns a shop, or an app developer dreaming of glory, people are on the lookout for ways to grow.

Ashoka was the third emperor of the Mauryan Dynasty in India. In the 3rd century BCE, it was one of the world's largest empires. He was not content. He was not like a lion, who attacks when he is hungry. He is not like an addict, who steals when he needs drugs. As is customary, he attacks because he wants more. He attacks because he can.

He attacked Kalinga, the neighboring kingdom. He knew he would win. His armies marched across the frontier. They crushed the defenders, mowed down every fighter, slaughtered every one of the wounded, soaking the ground. He expected a happy day. But as he surveyed the battlefield he was overcome with horror, revulsion, remorse.

He waded through the bloody fields, the bodies of a hundred thousand enemy soldiers, their horses and elephants, lifeless, twisted, in pieces and piles, and saw his conquest covered with decay and death.

He reflected on his vast, new empire, now reaching across northern India. He thought about what it could be. He devoted the wealth of his kingdom to virtue – non-violence, benevolence and peace. His empire recovered and flourished. It endured for centuries. His rock edicts – 30 carved pillars erected in what are now India, Pakistan, Nepal and Afghanistan – are still standing. They are inscribed with the message from him, King Ashoka, to the people, as a guide to a new way of life, intended to grow a society both wholesome and great, a new order for the ages, a complete break with the cruelty and darkness of the past.

With his support these vital ideas and values spread from Mauryan India, and flourished in the areas that are now Pakistan and Afghanistan, Russia, Central Asia, China, Tibet, Japan, Thailand, Burma, Mongolia, Viet Nam, Cambodia, Malaysia, Indonesia and beyond.

Genghis Khan

Genghis Khan united the warring tribes and nations of Mongolia, in the 13th century. He was the second son of a murdered chief. He and his mother and his brother were cast out of the tribal land, to starve.

They say his name should be pronounced Chinggis not Genghis. That when he was young he was called Temujin. Lots is known about the language of his time. What he did was recorded in the 13th century <u>Secret History of the Mongols</u>. Those secrets are out, but what was going on in his mind remains to be discovered. His mindset matters, because it seems to be filling the world, and heading this way.

His dad was murdered in a gang war, when little Temujin was too young to understand but not too young to be sad, hurt and enraged. Before his dad was killed his world made sense. It wasn't perfect, but it was good.

After his dad was killed, outside the safety and order of community life, all was isolated, barren and hard. The only people he loved were hungry, angry and alone.

The mindset that drove his conquest was savage, greedy, delighting in power and the suffering of others. That is the way of the world. Sometimes its reined in. Sometimes it runs loose. It is running loose now. Human settlements, cities and towns from sea to sea, are under siege. Once they were safe and orderly.

They did not always exist. They grew. They were built by people who came from far away, self-selected for confidence and drive. Most, by choice or circumstance, were fully committed to their new life. There was really no way back for them. The cities blossomed: the banks invested, the businesses prospered, the land was abundant, the work was plentiful. The people built new houses, wide boulevards, and manicured parks where you could go for a walk after work or hear a brass band concert on the weekend. The children went to school for free and learned what they would need to know to stand on their own two feet.

They learned about the wonderful things that science was discovering, and what great people did. After school they could walk home, or run off for an adventure in the woods before dinnertime.

In the evenings community centers were busy, civic improvement groups met, people met at ball fields for pick-up games, and just to visit. On Sundays the churches were full, full of friends and family and neighbors, sharing a view of the world that grew naturally from the life that everybody shared. After a hard week's work, they stood back, took a breath, saw a bigger picture and a higher purpose, and they had a nice meal, together. It wasn't perfect. But it was good.

Now those cities are barren. The names are the same, but the meaning is different. The blossoms fell long ago. The roots decayed and the stems in the old rose gardens are thorny stalks. People who live in these cities feel cast out.

Many men, fathers and brothers and cousins and friends, have been murdered. Many boys left angry and alone. Raised by women, lonely, agitated and afraid, whose authority is uneven. Whose care and kindness are worn thin. The boys are unhappy, weak, humiliated, angry and alone. They venture out. There they get taunted. They get the shit beat out of them. They band together. The gangs run the streets. They want to be a part of that. They get beat in. They get sent out to prove themselves – to beat someone and steal their stuff and bring it back as a trophy, a sign of competence, a payment and a commitment to the gang. They receive grudging approval. They are the new guys. They still have a lot to prove.

The world around them may be ugly but there is plenty out there. The smart ones calculate, manipulate, threaten, bribe, charm and intimidate.

They move ahead. And like anyone else who joins a big organization – a corporation, a team, a mafia, a military, a religious organization or a cartel

– it may begin the inevitable next step, or in self-interest, as an expedient, a way ahead. But soon enough, to get ahead, they embrace the values and the means and methods of the group, and they do get ahead. So, it should come as no surprise that a culture in decay and disorder will take rebirth in rage, and that a new order, based on blood and power, would arise. That is not unique. It has happened again and again. It is one way that people respond to circumstances.

Genghis, when he was still Temujin, was angry. And frustrated. He was always competing with his older brother. And his older brother, bigger, stronger, more experienced, had the advantage and won, again and again.

So, when Temujin caught a nice fish to eat, to fill his hungry stomach, to bring home to show his mom, and his brother stole the fish from him, he cut his throat. He deserved to die.

No more being humiliated, angry or alone for little Temujin.

His mom was angry. Not hard to understand. But on balance, he thought, he did the right thing. And it worked.

As a boy his marriage was arranged to a girl named Borte. As a young teen, by the time of their marriage, he loved her. But trouble finds its way into every life. A rival gang showed up, raided his tent, grabbed his girl, threw her on the back of a horse, rode away and disappeared over the horizon. There are a lot of fish in the sea. But fuck that. So, he got a few of his friends and went after her. A few nights later, when the raiding gang was on the move, carrying cartloads of stolen stuff and women,

Temujin and his friends made their way through the jostling caravan, searching for Borte. Easy to say. Most people would not have much experience moving through the darkness in the wild in the presence of an enemy who would instantly and happily kill you if they saw you. Just hiding from an enemy like that would be a mind-searing challenge for most.

Even running from them would be terrifying. Going into their midst in the middle of the night with just a few of your boys takes balls so big it would take a dump truck to move them, as they say. Which Temujin had. Which it took to grab Borte back from the warlord who stole her for himself, and to ride out of that crowd and disappear into the night. A hostage-rescue spec ops mission, with horses instead of helicopters.

Pretty soon everyone heard the story. He got the girl. And all the guys wanted to be his pal.

He formed a cavalry numbering in the hundreds of thousands, using a personnel policy which was novel for the steppes but had been effective across the middle east and North Africa for centuries: He staffed his army based on merit instead of family connections. Instead of killing the soldiers in the armies he defeated he invited the conquered soldiers to join him.

He rewarded his cavalry with inconceivable wealth. He threatened every city he came to, and slaughtered multitudes.

Sometimes, when besieging a city, he would release a handful of captives, knowing that, free, they would run to the next city and tell them, with a convincing breathless, first-person, blood drenched, eye-witness account of the death and destruction that would rain down upon them, and that only way out was complete submission. Genghis conquered by force and terror. He led by threats and promises.

The Mongols raided settled peoples. The cities hid treasures. The farmers their food and tended herds. They both were tied to the land, as were their armies. Most of these settled people ate several times a day, as most people do. The Mongols did not.

The Mongols were able to move at terrific and terrifying speeds because they could live on horseback, without stopping, without foraging, without a supply chain, and without supplies.

They could ride for days because they were tough enough and motivated enough to do it;

and if the bag of food they carried ran out they would cut a vein in the neck of their horse and sip his blood as they rode.

They deepened their understanding of the ways of war from their enemies' tactics: how to use diplomacy and deal-making, how to send spies to gather intelligence, to construct relay stations to speed communication, to split large enemy forces into small groups they could destroy. They used stealth and speed to appear out of nowhere; they became adept at using fear; they used innovative engineering to build siege engines to knock down city walls. They diverted rivers to deprive the besieged cities of water. They engulfed tribes, cities, nations and empires, from central Europe to the Pacific Coast of China.

Genghis cleared the ground with conquest. But to unify, administer and grow his empire he created a large bureaucracy, a new written language, a written code of law; he prosecuted corruption and bribery, and offered opportunity for the willing and able.

He left his unconquered 130,000-man army to his sons when he died.

A young Venetian merchant named Marco Polo met Genghis Khan's grandson and heir Kublai Khan at the Mongol's summer court in Shangdu, also called Xanadu. Marco Polo, along with his uncle and his dad, sailed from Venice and walked across Turkey, Central Asia and China to the Pacific Ocean, and back – Marco made the trip twice – travelling almost all the way on Mongol-controlled land, carrying a solid gold all-access pass, bearing the Imperial Seal of the Great Khan himself. They followed the roads and caravan routes known as The Silk Road.

Kublai Khan was not satisfied with his conquest of China. It was not enough. So, he sent a fleet of ships east over the Pacific Ocean, to attack Japan. Three times he attacked and three times the Mongol navy was blown back from Japan by storms known as the "kame kaze" – the divine winds – which protected Japan from Mongol conquest.

Undefeated masters of Bu, Kublai Khan's Mongol Chinese empire, known as the Yuan Dynasty, excelled in Bun as well. They took power, and they held on to it. They operated their Chinese empire in Chinese style. It was the Mongols, foreign conquerors, who instituted the Chinese government civil service exam, based on the native Chinese neo-Confucian "Four Books."

Passing this exam, and mastering the curriculum on which it was based, was the quintessential Chinese intellectual achievement. The exam prep was used for 700 years as the national educational curriculum, as a vehicle to promote unified values and knowledge, and as a merit-based mechanism to select the best and the brightest of Chinese society for government service. It was initiated by Kublai Khan's regime, a visionary implementation of Bun.

Where the Mongol army moved havoc and death followed. But then, order and prosperity grew from the smoking ruins. Bu and Bun.

And yet, within the span of one human life, three generations of leaders, the Mongol empire was dissolving. Kublai ruined his health with pleasure. His empire dissipated too. The Yuan Dynasty collapsed from disease, bankruptcy, military overreach, and mass migration.

Kublai was brilliant in war and peace. But he seemed to think his position at the apex of the world was his to keep.

George Washington

Like Alexander, Genghis, Kublai and Ashoka, George Washington led an audacious fight against great power. In his case it was not a contest for world domination. At least it didn't start that way. In case you have not heard much about this: Washington led a small-scale colonial rebellion against the British Empire, a global superpower of the 18th century.

For years, under his generalship, the American rebels lost battle after battle. They froze. They starved. They went broke. They persisted.

George Washington's guerilla forces had no doubt that their alternatives were victory or death. If frostbite and hunger were the price, then okay, you do what you have to do. One famous story has them walking all day and then all through the freezing night, circling to the undefended rear of the British camp, sniping from the cover of the woods, appearing and disappearing, and soon routing the large, well-equipped, well-trained, well-paid regular British army.

They were outnumbered, determined and brave. The Americans risked everything, held back nothing, and prevailed.

General Tariq Ibn Ziyad commanded his army to **"Burn the ships"** when his 7,000-man invasion force landed on the Mediterranean coast of Spain.

He was facing an opposing army of 100,000. What better way to encourage his men than the choice of victory or death? That was the year 711.

Conquistador Hernan Cortes, for the same reason, ordered his ships scuttled when his small force landed on the coast of Mexico (1519). They say Aeneas did it too, thousands of years before, after crossing the Aegean Sea to assault the land that would become Rome.

"Break the kettles and sink the ships!" was the order of the Qin army General at the battle of Julu, in the 2nd century BC. Advantageous though it is, giving 100% does not guarantee victory. He lost the war, the nation, and 200,000 men.

Competent Generals will not know the outcome of a battle in advance, but they will know when they have crossed the Rubicon. For the American revolutionaries that moment came with the Declaration of Independence of 1776, which spelled out the war aims and the rationale for rebellion. Benjamin Franklin, one of the signers, is quoted as saying:

"We must hang together or surely we will hang separately."

Any fighter will recognize this moment: In a confrontation a moment comes when there is no way out, no way to avoid, escape, de-escalate, or negotiate. At some point action is all.

George Washington reached that point. From Brooklyn to Valley Forge to Trenton to Saratoga, conditions changed. The rebels learned the lessons of asymmetrical warfare: how a small determined force can appear from nowhere, hit the enemy, and disappear like water into sand or smoke in the wind, earning victory by a thousand cuts.

The British military and political leadership in 18th century North America were, like dinosaurs, well-adapted to conditions that no longer existed.

What followed the unexpected American victory in the North American war was a decade long effort to formulate a peace that might endure.

The solution was the US Constitution. The Constitution set out the rules of order, and the relations of power, well enough to stabilize the nation, harmonize divergent interests, and function effectively for more than a hundred and fifty years.

The same people that fought the war turned their hearts and minds to statecraft after the war was won; shifting focus from Bu to Bun.

Bun has no Resting Place

As the Constitutional Convention concluded in 1787, the story goes, a lady stopped one of the delegates, Benjamin Franklin, as he was leaving. She asked about the new American Constitution: **"Well Doctor, what have we got, a republic or a monarchy?"** Franklin answered **"A republic. If you can keep it."**

As thinker and author Myron Magnet observed: **No constitution, however wisely designed⋯ can protect a people against tyranny or conquest if it weakens itself by unchecked "corruption of morals, profligacy of manners, and listlessness for the preservation of the natural and unalienable rights of mankind."**

That is the critical "Bun" component of Bun Bu Ryo Do. It is not fixed, soft, or literary. If you follow Napoleon – blazing through Austerlitz, freezing in Moscow – you can observe the consequences of its omission. Peace requires strength and virtue.

Bun Bu as a Trinity

Bun Bu Ryo Do is sometimes regarded as a binary system –
with the arts of war and of civil life ideally complementing each other in dynamic tension. In the 19th century Prussian General Karl von Clausewitz' cast war as "politics by other means."

This can be seen in the obverse as well: civil administration and social organization may be conducted as "war by other means." If advantage and fear are the guiding principles of civil life, there is oppression. There is a misguided view of both war and peace.

Bun Bu Ryo Do is not a binary system. It is a trinity: the arts of war, the arts of peace and the path we travel as we use them. All the parts are changing all the time.

That is why we martial artists continue to train for a lifetime.

The Bun Bu Trinity: Tactics, Ethics, Metaphysics

"Tactics" in the broad sense includes more than fighting: Techniques, training, operations, strategy, logistics, mission, morale, communication, planning, technology, transport, intelligence, and leadership are all essential components of any tactical engagement – personal, corporate, or national.

Our choice of tactics, and our ability to employ them effectively, in the dojo, in combatives and otherwise, depends on an accurate knowledge of how things work.

That consists of more than knowledge of manpower, firepower, maneuver, terrain and the other observable characteristics of the battlespace. Understanding "how things work" requires an accurate understanding of minds and metaphysics.

Metaphysics

For example, if we understand that cause and effect are continually in operation – that everything we see has causes and that everything we do has effects –

and if we understand that everything and everyone is continually changing – then we can examine which causes produce which effects and choose to act in ways which are most likely to fulfill our goals.

That is a metaphysical insight – the validity of cause & effect and of impermanence & change – which we can use, in action.

If we choose an erroneous metaphysic – like the view that "everything is a crapshoot," a matter of chance, or "life sucks and then you die," or "it's all about feeling good," or "whoever dies with the most stuff wins" – then our choices will reflect our view, and sooner or later life will come crashing down, like the total loss of a hopeless gambler, a washed-up racketeer, or a tyrannical state.

Dojo Application

If we understand change and causality then we can look at a kata and see deeply: which attack would need which defense; what new targets might be exposed as a result, what counters might then be applied, how those counters themselves might be foiled, and how we might make the most of the new permutation, and so on, until the threat is resolved.

The kata cannot be interpreted as if the techniques were like a row of dominoes, falling predictably in sequence. We can do a thorough analysis in the dojo, from multiple points of view with multiple possible outcomes. A skilled martial artist can put these insights into action, in kumite or in combatives. This application in the heat of the moment happens faster than cognition. But it happens.

This endlessly changing "rock, paper, scissors" dynamic has been described in terms of "five-phase" wu-hsing theory, the eight ba gua, the I Ching, and by other symbol systems, esoteric and otherwise – but the premise that transformation is continuous, patterned and caused – is consistent throughout all these systems. And so is the implication that if you can understand how the transformations work then you can employ them to your advantage.

The principles of cause & effect, and patterns of continual change, applies to every part of every life.

Ethics

Accurate metaphysical understanding – insight into the way things exist – is only accessible to us if our minds are clear and stable; and our minds will only be clear and stable if we have good relationships with others. People who lie, steal, cheat, rape and kill to get what they want, do not get to think clearly. If you have spent even a little time with people who live this way you can tell.

Having meaningful, good relationships with people is a matter of mutual responsibility as well as of affection and respect.

Close relationships require courage – tenderness, the strength to do what is right, and the power to defend ourselves and others, when the time comes. All good relationships require us to treat people fairly and honestly, considering their well-being not just our own. Without disciplined, ethical behavior the mind becomes overwrought – stressed, scheming, paranoid, occupied by fear and desire.

Strong dojos grow where people challenge each other and collaborate. Then skills improve. People get strong, confident and honest. Dojos dissolve when people are disrespectful, arrogant and servile. When people deceive and exploit each other. Just like families, nations, and lives.

No matter how strong you are, or who you dominate, or how much you take, it will all slip away, if force is all you have to work with. Every successful leader knows that you rely on your people to reach your objectives. You can rely on them if you respect them, share with them, see to their well-being. If you take them for granted or cut them out, if you rely on threats and bribes, eventually they will turn against you. As they should.

Tyrants and gangsters fighting their way up to the top of the heap by any means necessary all fall, in a collapse that will likely be beyond any limit they ever imagined.

The Unified Field of Action

As martial artists our ethics, tactics and metaphysics are not separate realms. They are the three-dimensional universe in which we act. The Bun, Bu and Do. The deeper we penetrate into one of these dimensions, the deeper the implications for mastering the others. Using them we can build a life that is good and strong. We can leave a legacy that will endure.

In this unified field of action we can be

> "…as swift as wind, as gentle as the forest, as fierce as fire, as firm as a mountain…"

in a poetic expression of this martial, human ideal.

***

Killing People and Taking their Stuff

So, it seems that killing people and taking their stuff has been popular throughout history. Many great historical figures are considered great for doing this. Empires have been built on it. Sun Tzu, military genius, guide for every military in the modern world, taught how to do it, although he recommends taking people's stuff without killing them, if possible. Clausewitz' "War is politics by other means," expresses the view that the chief interest of the state is power. Whether it is furthered through diplomatic persuasion or military violence is a matter of expedience.

Alexander the Great, Genghis Khan, and Napoleon were not unusual people, at least not with regard to their values. In that they were common. They were coveting at an unusual scale, but the feeling was widely shared.

That is how they assembled great armies and focused the energies of their confederates on their neighbors.

Read the history of empires as they grew and you will see this ethos in operation. In Europe and throughout the Americas, the middle east, north Africa, central Asia, and the east. It did not begin a few centuries ago. Its origins are untraceable; but they can be traced to the earliest evidence, before human settlements, where piles of hand axes, fragments of broken ribs and shattered femurs tell the tale.

Out of all the things that people can do, many have thought this to be the best. It is popular right now. On the borders of nations and within nations, in homeless camps, apartments and houses, on backroads and city streets, its popular. Breaking and entering, fraud, threats and assault are all popular. And what about all the reports in the news of an "armed robbery gone wrong?" We don't hear much about the armed robberies gone right, but they are popular too. The frauds, exactions, and intricate associations of powerful intercessors extract their cuts unobserved, but with force and the threat of force near at hand.

In gang wars, in piracy ancient and modern, in the competitive strategies and internal policy of cartels, globally and locally, killing people and taking their stuff are the means and the motive.

Doing them effectively is a key compensation metric for the HR departments of all criminal organizations, a core competence, and a pillar of their business model. That is not new.

It has been justified as a fight for glory. A fight for "us". As revenge. As the answer to "Why not?" As the self-evident truth "Better us than them." It has been declared divine right. The mandate of heaven. Manifest destiny. Darwin vindicated. Creation of global order. The path to peace. Inevitable progress.

People have justified its righteousness because "they have a lot, while we have a little." Because "they have become weak while we have grown strong." It has been justified as the fight for right. As our turn. Because we will do unto others what was done unto us before, or what might be done to us if we don't.

Ardent proponents declare that the goal must be achieved by any means necessary. For the revolution. For the triumph of the will. For lebensraum. As the path to the Pax Whatever.

But here and there, in the valley of the shadow of death, in the presence of enemies great and small, named and nameless, grew countless counter-movements. Some withered. Some flourished. Some prevailed. Some became great forces of history.

Our training grows from them. From the defenders of boats and beaches, fields and towns on Okinawa long ago, from Japan and China, to here and now. From Pacific atolls, across the Americas to Europe's Atlantic shore. A response to battered walls and burning fields a thousand years ago; a response to the fevered pleas and curses blistering the world's cities last night.

It grew from the wish not to be killed. Not to have our families, friends and neighbors incinerated, intimidated, threatened or hurt.

To keep our lives and livelihoods intact: our homes and land and all the things that we and those who came before us worked for and built, treasured and protected.

From the wish to keep everyone safe and well.

To keep them safe and well may mean giving up safety and well-being, and taking on responsibility and hardship. To get strong and skillful. To be righteous and vigilant, and to stay that way until the threat disappears or is overcome. Which may be never.

Which might be good. To stay strong and vigilant is a good way to live.

Threats and pressures, from inconvenient to mortal, appear in every life. Whatever form they take, we will be more prepared to take them on because we train the way we do.

A purposeful and courageous life cannot be manufactured, inherited, bought or stolen. It must be built, one at a time, by hand.

***

From Buddha to OODA

Bunkai: Tactics not just Techniques

Some martial artists who claim to be teaching "the warrior way" seem unaware of what warriors do. The reciprocation of training and experience – between the arena of training on the one hand and of the street or battlefield on the other – generated the martial culture of medieval Japan, and on Okinawa, as they have in the west. Both training and experience are the indispensable sources for combative professionals today. They form the foundation on which we build our martial art. Without either one of these, martial arts can be neither martial nor art.

Some martial arts groups only access information from within their own organization. Their knowledge-base will shrink in every generation in which it persists, as practitioners move further in time and in experience from the practical combative vitality and jeopardy that forged their arts.

You can observe this disconnect between "traditional" martial arts and combatives in bunkai interpretation.

Bunkai has advanced from the primitive "everything is a block and a punch" of years ago, the days when three "knife hand chest blocks" in a row stopped three punches from an attacker taking three backward steps. Or when a "high block" finished the fight because the attacker got a broken arm from your high block and ran away.

But there is more to do. The basis of lots of current bunkai analysis is still the question "What is my opponent doing to elicit this move in the kata?" – as a way to understand what the kata is trying to teach. That is a reactive model that makes assumptions about distances, speed, and rules which do not correspond to chaotic combative dynamics. There is a lot we can know, and rely on, for sound, practical interpretation. The presumption of single combat, energy output at a constant rate without accounting for bursts or fatigue, and stand-alone knockout techniques – are not realistic and will limit the spectrum of interpretation.

It does not appear that kata are a catalog of techniques. That's a good start. But sound kata analysis needs to include tactics. This is supported by combative experience and accounts for key aspects of the design of the kata. There also appear to be training components in kata which may not themselves be tactical, but which extend our tactical abilities beyond our natural strengths, for example, by having us do techniques and combinations leading with both left and right.

Every technique we do has counters. Every technique we do exposes targets. We need to be able to respond to any of the counters for each technique we launch, and consider how we will follow up. We need to train to be able to exploit every vulnerability that our opponent's choice of technique exposes. We also have to prepare for a decisive follow up if our technique fails. Bunkai analysis should be on the lookout for this.

Here is another tactical point that is often overlooked in bunkai analysis: At high pressure, under sudden attack, one essential response in the tool kit has to be the ability to break contact in order to terminate the attacker's momentum, and then to immediately re-engage as the aggressor. This is typical in boxing and kumite, but may be omitted from bunkai interpretation.

The opponent's attack attempts to establish the momentum of the encounter. To retake the momentum, you may need to quickly disengage and then re-engage. This accounts for some of the body shifting and footwork which appear in the kata.

With this in mind we can understand that the kata is teaching how to retake the initiative, dominate, and recover the momentum of the fight. This is why we use a side step and turn for a flanking counterattack. It may be one of several reasons why we reverse direction while our visual focus remains in the same direction.

Making a habit of covering your six instantly, is another piece of tactical training sometimes overlooked in bunkai interpretation, but evident in the embusen of kata.

Recognizing the vulnerabilities of each posture and technique, and making a habit of defending them, appears in kata. Countering a counterattack, when your move has been unsuccessful in stopping the opponent, is built into kata. These are indispensable skills in practical combatives. In contact things don't go as planned.

Without experience we may be unaware of these aspects of encounters, miss these components in kata, and overlook the training opportunity for self-defense application. Without this we will miss what is encoded in the kata, and so miss the chance to do karate kata as they are designed, as practical training.

For Honor, Glory and Victory

16th century Japanese warrior Miyamoto Musashi fought 60 sword combat duels, challenges, mostly as tests of skill. He was undefeated. Many of his adversaries died.

At the end of his life he wrote about what he had learned.

Warriors put their lives at risk for honor – the reputation for fearlessness – and for glory – being known as the best. He was both. His Book of Five Rings has been influential in the thinking and practice of warriors, and others, ever since.

Warriors still put their lives on the line, in the same way, for the same reasons, not only in battle but in competitive challenge. During his life as a fighter pilot and trainer John Boyd took on hundreds of challengers in potentially lethal aerial combat training. He was supremely confident and, as the lead combat instructor at the United States Air Force's most elite fighter school, was continually challenged by young, ambitious, brilliantly talented pilots. He was never defeated. He was like Musashi, but with more experience.

In his time as an F-100 fighter pilot and instructor at Nellis Air Force Base, during the Korean War era, 889 F-100s were destroyed in accidents; 324 F-100 pilots died. In accidents. In training. These pilots challenged one another and their instructors, they challenged themselves and their weapons, to achieve victory in every engagement. These were not combat casualties. The challenges were real. Boyd could have been one of them, any day. He wasn't. Like Musashi, John Boyd wrote about what he learned. His insights and his writing changed the way war is fought worldwide; his work is as influential as Sun Tzu's <u>Art of War</u>.

While his specific insights into weapons are relevant mostly to military aviation, his theory of combat has become a standard component of training in law enforcement and military academies, worldwide. Not only do his insights keep people alive, his description of the decision-making process fighters use in combat has been applied to business, game theory, computing, sports, warfare on the strategic and tactical level – and many others.

These insights have high relevance in martial arts. They will provide advantage to fighters, competitors and practitioners who use them.

The path from Buddha to OODA runs through Budo

Both the modern US military and medieval Japanese military recognized two critical areas of concern in combative training:

1. techniques and tactics, and 2. condition of mind and body.

Both needed to solve the same problem – to overcome the will of an opponent who is using violence to defeat you.

In both the conventional wisdom was falling behind the times. In both cultures the key tactical innovators were supreme experts in single combat, whose insights were extended to operational and strategic fighting.

Take a look at how closely these excerpts below, drawn from key sources of thought in modern warfare and Japanese Zen-budo, track with each other. See if what they say speaks to the heart of what we do in martial arts.

One source is Warfighting – a hundred-page book that conveys the official fighting doctrine of the US Marine Corps. Warfighting is based in large part on John Boyd's principles of maneuver warfare, also known as Fourth Generation warfare.

The second source below is from Takuan Soho, 16th century Japanese Zen priest and the teacher of Yagyu Munenori, the founder of one of the great sword-fighting schools of samurai era Japan, an instructor and adviser to the Shogun.

Takuan, like Boyd and Musashi, was a leading influencer of combative theory. Despite their distance in time, place and culture, they arrive at very similar conclusions regarding the keys to victory and the primacy of the mind in combat. They identified the same errors. In some respects, they recommend the same remedies.

As modern martial artists, in the Okinawan tradition or otherwise, we can make use of the insights from medieval Japan and advanced modern warfare in what we do. We can see that some of the principles of combat with a three-foot blade, a 25-ton fighter jet, or body weapons are the same.

The modern and medieval approaches sound different.
Not just because they are written in different languages. Each uses the terminology, categories and worldview drawn from the most highly regarded sources of truth in their cultures. For the educated, ruling elite in samurai era Japan, the most comprehensive and most reliable source of truth were the great philosophical and religious texts of the Buddhist, Taoist and Confucian traditions imported from China. Takuan prefaces his thought about swordsmanship with reference to the Kegon Kyo or Avatamsaka Sutra – the primary text of the Chinese Hua Yen school.

Boyd, and contemporary warfighters who draw on his insights today, speak the language of STEM. In modern, educated, elite society here and now science, technology, engineering and mathematics provide the description of reality considered most real, most useful, and most true. In our culture a preponderance of resources go to support institutions and individuals who operate within this world view.

Talented people are drawn to it. For them, it is the best way to understand the world, to identify what matters, and to get the results they want.

STEM language and sutra language are parallel cultural structures. They inform the thinking of their elites in a parallel way: their language, ideas and values are applied to the dynamics of power. They are not the same thought systems. But as applied to combatives they identify the same issues, and their analysis yielded results which correspond very closely, and which we can use.

Then and Now

Takuan: Ignorance is written with characters meaning "no enlightenment" and refers to confusion. A state of fixation is written with characters meaning a "state of lingering."

Warfighting: Decision making may be an intuitive process based on experience⋯ We should base our decisions on awareness rather than on mechanical habit.

Takuan: The moment you see an opponent come with a cutting stroke, if you think of parrying it right then and there, your mind lingers on the opponent's sword that way, so you fail to act in time; thus you get killed by the opponent.

Warfighting: Inherent in maneuver warfare is the need for speed to seize the initiative, dictate the terms of action, and keep the enemy off balance, thereby increasing his friction. We seek to establish a pace that the enemy cannot maintain so that with each action his reactions are increasingly late—until eventually he is overcome by events.

Takuan: Whether an opponent attacks or you attack, if you fix your mind on the attacker, the attacking sword, the pace or the rhythm, even for a moment, your own actions will be delayed, and you'll be killed.

Warfighting: Whenever possible, we exploit existing gaps. Failing that, we create gaps. Due to the fluid nature of war, gaps will rarely be permanent and will usually be fleeting. To exploit them demands flexibility and speed.

Takuan: Zen master Hui-neng said: If you understand the teaching of immediacy, you do not cultivate practice grasping externals; you simply activate accurate perception at all times.

Warfighting: War is inherently disorderly, and we cannot expect to dictate its terms with any sort of precision··· commanders gain the initiative, preserve momentum, and control the tempo of operations.

Compare this observation to experience in kumite:

Warfighting: Tempo is often associated with a mental process known variously as the "decision cycle," "OODA loop," or "Boyd cycle" ···Boyd identified a four-step mental process: observation, orientation, decision, and action. Boyd theorized that each party to a conflict first observes the situation. On the basis of the observation, he orients; that is, he makes an estimate of the situation. On the basis of the orientation, he makes a decision. Finally, he implements the decision—he acts. Because his action has created a new situation, the process begins anew. Boyd argued that the party who consistently completes the cycle faster gains an advantage that increases with each cycle. His enemy's reactions become increasingly slower by comparison and therefore less effective until, finally, he is overcome by events."

(This occurs on the scale of microseconds.)

···Harry Hillaker (chief designer of the F-16) said of the OODA theory:

"Time is the dominant parameter. The pilot who goes through the OODA cycle in the shortest time prevails because his opponent is caught responding to situations that have already changed···."

The same advantage holds for martial artists.

"… The key to survival and autonomy is the ability to adapt to change, not perfect adaptation to existing circumstances. Indeed, Boyd noted that radical uncertainty is a necessary precondition of physical and mental vitality: all new opportunities and ideas spring from some mismatch between reality and ideas about it…"

This has important implications for the way martial artists fight, but also in how we train. If there is no room for innovation, challenge, proof and transformation, martial arts lose vitality in training and effectiveness in application.

Compare this to target selection in empty hand and kobudo:

Warfighting: (paraphrased) Given the historical conditions in which he fought and theorized, 19th century Prussian General von Clausewitz advocated applying maximum force against the enemy's center of gravity – his strongest mass of forces – to deliver the decisive blow. "…daring all to win all."

Today however the theory of modern maneuver warfare is much closer to the tactical approach of the martial artist.

Warfighting: "We have since come to prefer pitting strength against weakness." ⋯we apply our force to the enemy's critical vulnerability.

In exploiting "suki" – fleeting gaps in the opponent's defense and attention, and "kyusho" – weak points in the opponent's body structure, we also recognize the advantage of applying power to vulnerability.

It is significant that before Boyd used calculus, physics and engineering to analyze and describe aerial maneuvers pilots believed their tactics were an ineffable function of feeling – intuitive and fundamentally mysterious.

This is the way mushin is regarded by some now in the martial arts world⋯ and may account for their objection to my comparison of mushin with "flow" states as described in the neurobiology and psychology of high performance in sports and other human endeavors.

The fact that we can understand what we are doing makes it possible for us to be more accomplished and more effective. It does not reduce the beauty or depth of our art. It does not profane the sacred.

While this does not resolve the claim that ultimate liberation is a necessary concomitant of ultimate technical mastery, modern martial artists who apply the insights of warriors, ancient and modern, directly to kata, kata interpretation and practical combatives, have an advantage.

*

Note: Quotes credited above are from:
-Takuan Soho, The Inscrutable Subtlety of Immoveable Wisdom, 1573-1645, translated by Thomas Cleary, hosted on Terebess.
-John Boyd's presentation "A Discourse on Winning and Losing: The Patterns of Conflict" – unpublished lecture notes and diagrams, August, 1987.

-Warfighting, 1997, Marine Corps Doctrinal Publication 1. This edition incorporates the Marine Corps' maneuver warfare doctrine. The author of the 1989 original publication Fleet Marine Force Manual – 1 (FMFM-1) is Captain John Schmitt.

***

Karate and Nuclear War

Shoshin Nagamine, founder of Matsubayashi Ryu Karate, was a Police Chief and an Okinawan political official for much of his life.

He was also recognized for his spiritual achievements. In his address "Karate and World Peace" he reflected on the spiritual heritage of Okinawan culture, as embodied in karate, and its role in the recovery following World War II.

In December 1996, Nagamine Shoshin traveled to Hawaii to receive acknowledgment of his Zen realization – Ken Zen Ichi Nyo (Karate and Zen as One) from the Archbishop of Daihonzan Chozen-ji, the 84th Dharma Successor of Rinzai Zen. The quotes below, in bold, are from the speech he gave at the testimonial dinner in his honor, in recognition of his commitment to world peace through the way of karate.

He said **"There is a Ryukyu chant which reads: 'In a world full of conflict and strife, do not cry over the condition of the world, your life is the treasure.'"**

He explained that Okinawan martial philosophy was not bushido, which in its 20th century militarist iteration, devalued life. On the contrary, he said, the Okinawan martial ideal is devoted to life.

Shoshin Nagamine lived through the "Typhoon of Steel", the months-long Battle of Okinawa fought between the Allies and Japan in 1945, during which a third of the people of Okinawa and many others, hundreds of thousands, were killed.

Those Okinawans who remained alive were impoverished, overwhelmed by shock and grief.

Shoshin Nagamine's revival of karate, and its unique spirit and philosophy, helped restore the health, hope and dignity of the people in the years following the war.

In the historical perspective, a key factor of a nation being able to enjoy a healthy growth has been to maintain culture in one hand and martial arts in the other hand. That is, maintaining both of the above was critical in governing a nation. – Shoshin Nagamine

Shoshin Nagamine is referring to "Bun Bu Ryo Do" – "the way of both civil culture and martial skill." For a leader – as for every responsible adult – the capacity for both civic virtue and martial skill, and the knowledge of when to apply them – is indispensable.

As a karate practitioner, career law enforcement officer, government official and noted community leader, Shoshin Nagamine lived this ethos.

The judicious use of force employed to protect innocent people, to maintain social order and justice, requires that we cultivate the martial and the civil in our own lives.

I truly hope that the people in the world would change their mind-set of aggression and first-strike to a philosophy of karate ni sente nashi. It is only through this philosophy that world peace will be achieved. – Shoshin Nagamine

Literally translated "Karate ni sente nashi" says "Fists that do not strike first" or "Not hitting first". A deeper extension of the translation is "the fists that give life", According to a note by translator Hideyuki Takahashi.

Karate Ni Sente Nashi

Shoshin Nagamine saw the misery that results from arrogance and aggression. Instead of glory and triumph it brought degradation and death, which like an oil slick on the sea, spread and poisoned everything it touched.

He devoted his life and his vision to restoring the happiness of his people.

He helped to create a peaceful renewed society which, by the 1950s and 60s, was rising from the ashes of the Second World War.

As a reminder: the Second World War was in part a nuclear war. But not like the nuclear war being contemplated by important people today. Then, in the 1940s, there were only a few, primitive nukes, available only to one side.

In his talk "Karate and World Peace" Shoshin Nagamine reflected on the resilience of the Okinawan people under centuries of oppression following the Satsuma invasion in 1609 – a shocking change for them, after centuries of close, peaceful relations with imperial China. But as he explained this historical example he was not dreaming of battles of long ago. He was well aware that the fight for freedom continues:

I would like to emphasize here that Ryukyu people's resistance with respect to the issue of scaling down the size of United States armed forces in Okinawa is a good example of exercising the supreme right destined to Ryukyu people from the Heavens. The people of Okinawa would never be pushed back even if governing people try to force the issue. In the end, the resolve of the people will surface and press the governments of Japan and the United States into a corner by forcing a popular vote by the people. I have to say that both governments should be fully aware of this. People will not be fooled by a short-term political solution.

Near the end of his life Nagamine Shoshin was honored with the title "Japanese Living Treasure", in recognition of his achievements. His conviction that the will of the people will not be permanently suppressed has implications beyond Okinawa.

***

Making History

It may be that the modern world is in an advanced stage of decline. We don't need to decline with it. We are not helplessly riding an arc of history. History is not a thing. History is what people do.

We can think in accord with accepted norms or contrary to them. Or neither: we can make choices based on what is right. That includes what to do, where to go, which sights, sounds and ideas we engage with, who to have as friends.

Even as warnings proliferate there is time to prepare. In the moment of crisis, it will be too late. We train.

As a foundation for training, we live with gratitude. We appreciate our art, lives, work, friends and families. Anyone can criticize anyone. It takes no special discernment to find flaws in yourself or in other people. Anyone can complain. An attitude of dissatisfaction may masquerade as high standards but if it is a habit of negativity without remedy, it is vandalism. It may be an attempt to elevate oneself by leveling others. It may be an attempt to split friends apart to create factions. Whatever the motive: it is destructive – of the individuals involved and of the morale of the group. It is the corrosive inverse of gratitude.

We have a better way. When we detect a flaw, we remedy it. Where there is a deficiency, we add. Where there is excess, we reduce it. When there is no remedy, we change course and move on. There is work to do.

In the course of training, we will all overcome obstacles and opposition. There will be detours, sidetracks, missed chances and dry holes. But we recognize them for what they are and continue to move with purpose toward our goal.

Appreciate the foundation you have already built – the condition of your body, your mind, your heart, your will – and use all your spirit and energy, all your tools, all your gifts, include everyone who wants to join in, and build on it.

Be ready to be free. That is how history is made.

***

Conclusion

When I wrote the short essay which Sakiyama Sogen titled "True Karate Dō" I imagined that the ideals it expressed would make a complete dojo practice – training in virtue and mastering technique as wholesome worldly pursuits; training in transcendence as an ultimate goal - as a way to orient all the components of a life of practice.

This book outlines some of the steps I have taken over the years to construct a way of training that could make use of those high ideals.

I have reflected on the events and ideas again and again, like a kata, seeing more deeply over time. There is nothing you would see in our dojo that would look like philosophy, or mind training, or character development. You would see people getting strong, healthy and skillful.

How many dojos, meditation groups and many others, begin with daily practice, careful study, but then, almost effortlessly, turn their attention to marketing, membership drives, fund raising, social media and real estate.

That change is confusing. It is not obvious how to sustain a practice that is vital and genuine. A place of your own feels good and secure. It can be a tool, a source of validation, and a burden. Because, as everyone knows, whatever you own, pretty soon, starts to own you.

The best karate I have done, with the most accomplished practitioners, was in simple places. One was in a home dojo.

Another was in an appliance shop on the second floor of a building in the middle of nowhere. Another was in the meeting room of a once-busy church, with cracked walls and holes in the floor.

Wabi-sabi lives. Not just as a respite for the harried potentates of a brutal, golden age, long ago and far away.

Wabi-sabi is the old Japanese aesthetic of poverty and simplicity, of the imperfection and impermanence of the most beautiful things. An old Japanese tea house is peaceful, graceful, suspended in time, because of these qualities.

Monumental architecture evokes a very different set of values.

Hospital architecture has nothing to do with health or healing or well-being. It is a statement of power. Just like corporate headquarters, shopping malls, ancient temples, grand cathedrals, castles, and the vast public architecture of imperial states. They dwarf people. They entice you: enter here, unite with this power, disappear into this power. When children are afraid, they look to their parents for refuge. People seek refuge in power.

Sleek dojos are nice. The design of Zen temples can be exquisite. Where is our attention drawn?

What do we value most? What is the practice like? What are the people in them actually doing?

We can be enchanted by appearances. We can be seduced and manipulated by them. That includes the rarefied "simplicity" of gardens and tea houses and dojos, and the embracing, solid, soaring, holy grandeur of cathedrals. These are beautiful places. They change the feeling in your heart when you are there. You want to linger in them. Why is that?

Now, when life is dominated by crass urban architecture, hard, cold, square, haphazard, made for no one - beautiful places are a refuge, a retreat to Eden, to an imagined past and a possible future of dignity, harmony, a home for the natural, the sacred, a wholesome human life, in a vast, ordered cosmos. A dojo should feel like that. A life should.

Why do we get that feeling? Why do we want it so much?

There is a feeling you get after a long trek through the woods or a long drive through a wilderness when, off in the distance, you see a house, or a shed, or a barn, or a village. Even if it is a long way away, there is a primal echo in it.

It means something to you. You are drawn to it.

There is a feeling you get after being packed in a city, driving out, when you can start to see the world beyond – the sky getting bigger, a horizon, some woods, mountains appear, and vanish into the distance, far away.

Or you start to smell the ocean, the land flattens out and the trees get small, and then you see it. It opens up before you. It moves you. It awakens something. Serenity envelopes you. You have arrived somewhere.

People like to build houses at the beach and in the mountains. The view of a house from the wilderness is as pleasing as the view of the wilderness from a house. There is a reason for it and it is ancient and good and we use it every day in training.

Two geometries meet and play. The fractal geometry of the natural world – sea, clouds, desert, prairie, forest, mountains, trees – meets the Euclidean geometry of the world made by human hands, with straight lines, planes, cubes, cylinders and pyramids.

It is a contrast. The two geometries mean two different things to us and they evoke two separate landscapes of the mind.

The fractal world offers variation, exploration, discovery, a rough predictability mixed with danger and reward. The Euclidean means order, control, security and refuge. We need them both. For two million years of human history we had them both. This is no time to let them go.

The same juxtaposition of geometries makes hand-turned wooden bowls made from burls interesting. One look and we see the unpredictable under control. It looks nice, so we look closer. We investigate the details, examine the variations in the patterns, the repetition and surprise, all bounded and delineated in the dependable uniformity of the contours of the bowl, the strange, crude cancer of the tree redeemed and refined by the clever art of the craftsman.

By juxtaposing the two geometries we can explore while remaining oriented. That's what happens at a chalet, a hunting lodge, a beach house, a dacha, a farm, a yurt, a sod hut or a cabin. Head out and come back. Get cold and warm up. Face danger and escape. Hunt and return with your dinner. If you can.

Neither of the geometries is the privileged reality. Both are real. Both are compelling. Each derives meaning from the other. Like the burl:

To the tree it is a disease, to the lumberman it is a defect, to the artisan it is a treasure. What is it really? It is really all those. And more. To me the burl is an interesting metaphor. The burl "itself" does not have a nature separate from all those people and perspectives.

No-self nature is an odd expression but the example of the burl shows how familiar the concept is. The burl is a good example. It has no emotion attached to it, so we can think about it and shift perspective easily.

We exist this way too. That is why we have to decide what our lives are worth. If we don't someone else will. And what will they decide? What have they decided? Do the elite really see us as useless eaters, or as pockets of money to mine, or data points to be aggregated? To the machines we are no one. To your family you are wonderful and loved and essential. Who are you to you?

You can tell a lot about people from where they like to be. And what they do when they get there. We use the juxtaposition between familiarity and exploration in our dojo training, continually. Like fire and water, maintaining balance between the two is essential for using them well. But the balance is always changing.

Repetition of techniques juxtaposed with the exploration of their mechanics and their use. Training routines to make us fit and strong, mixed with variation in pressure, duration, new challenges and techniques, and from time to time, the shock of a new experience, unexpected, unfamiliar and indispensable for deep training.

We like the juxtaposition. Without it, we are stuck with rote repetition, robotic and dull. Or with excess variation which cannot produce skill training or high performance.

Continual exploration and deepening connection with our bodies, our minds, our training partners, our experience is essential to keep our art alive, our practice fruitful and our lives strong and good. And it makes each kata a cathedral, a tea house, a sea.

We venture out and we return, changed. On every scale. It applies to a lifetime, a life event, a year, a day at work, a career, having a family, getting a degree, doing a class, taking a breath, breathing your last.

Teenagers on Friday night grab the car keys and go. Can't wait. Somethings' is out there. Anything is possible. Later on, or early in the morning, they come home, ready to go to sleep. They need to do both.

Odysseus heads out to fight the raiders, overflowing with ambition, confidence and hunger for revenge. The mission doesn't go as planned. His army is destroyed.

But he lives. He is victorious.

He makes his way home. It takes ten years. He arrives home. It is still not over. He needs to wage war, to strategize, to deceive, to enlist his son, and to subdue a mass of scheming rivals.

Order must be restored. He has to do it. Persuasion will not work. It will need to be by force, against long odds, if he is ever to live peacefully and return to his rightful place in the world – to his home and family and people.

Like Frodo, leaving home and comfort, his breakfast of bread and butter, venturing out, into the shadow of death, not at all knowing what to expect or how to prepare, but willing to risk everything, to make the world better. To make the world not have to die.

And then, after long and desperate striving, victorious, hurt, he returns home to discover that things have changed there too, for the worse. He discovers that order and decency will need to be restored, there at home. By persuasion, if possible, by force if necessary.

The weak need protection from tyranny. The innocent need defense from exploitation. He discovers that if bun and bu are not kept in balance, like the pot warming in the hearth, then conflict is inevitable. Destruction and revolution will follow.

Then, in the way of the world, good people will be called upon to prevent this imbalance when they can, or to restore order when things have gone too far.

This cycle and this duty are not just for heroes. Not just for special people, who lived long ago, far away, whose stories are told, who are imaginary, and whose destinies we remember.

It is for all of us, every day. Heading out to the world to do what we need to do to make things good, to make things right, to make things work, to get what's ours and then to return home for rest and respite. And we all know that even there sometimes, after the school day, after the emails, after the phone calls, after the bills get opened and the news watched, even there the balance of loving kindness and strength is essential, peace and vigilance will be placed in balance, order preserved, protected or restored, before we rest.

Like a kata, beginning from the origin point, departing, fighting – with vigilance, effort and energy continuing until the battle is won.

Then, at the end of the kata, when the battle is done and we return to the origin point, we rest and recover but remain alert, because we are well aware that another kata will follow, another battle, another cycle of engagement, persistence, victory and rest.

We are changed because of what we wanted, what we faced and what we have done.

Then we begin again. We judge: is the change good or bad? Strengthening us or weakening us. Building up or tearing down? That's up to us. There is no automatic answer. Like the cycle of training and the cycle of lives. Like the fractal process of feeding back new information into the formula, changing one variable in each iteration, and creating something unexpected, new and yet familiar, as the process continues on and on. That is how kata training works. That is the how we train, to skill, to freedom.

This is what has led to the development of Yamabayashi Ryu – maintaining our orientation in the precisely preserved framework of kata, exploring in every dimension, continually, for a lifetime, sending down new roots, sending out new shoots, doing new research, so the style will live, grow, and flourish.

Now that we can see this, we can contemplate the relationship between the river of practice flowing on, unhindered, unbound, freely moving and adapting, with a purpose, to a goal, and clearly see the vortices of addiction, of attachment, of greed, anger and delusion which bind us, hinder us and keep us from moving on. We can really train. Really live.

As we do advanced training, we begin to see mujo - impermanence, ku - unsatisfactoriness, and kara – emptiness, directly – that is we see the transitory nature of things, that our lives are subject to continual restlessness, dissatisfaction, joy and pain, and that our lives are made of what we do.

That is why we need to decide what our lives are worth, right now.

You might not notice all these things at first when you have a look at what we are doing in our dojo. You will just see people, getting healthy and strong, learning to protect themselves, keep their minds sharp, moving skillfully after a long day's work, before heading out into the cool night breeze, for the ride home.

But that is the approach we take to training in our dojo, wherever that is, wherever we may be⋯

***

Part Five
Yamabayashi Ryu

Here are reflections on some important issues in training, all of which will be encountered, but may be unrecognized.

The Best Martial Art

We love our training. We know what it is, and what we get from it. Not everyone does. So, from time to time, we run into people who criticize karate. They say it is not as aggressive as this martial art, not as esoteric as that one, not as practical as that other martial art, not as morally virtuous as another, etc. They repeat the marketing claims of their styles. They want to feel good about what they do.

We don't spend time criticizing other arts, because ours is deep and great and gives us what we want – strength and speed, flexibility and endurance, mental clarity and confidence, practical self-defense skill and more.

Since the information in this book is addressed to practitioners of Yamabayashi Ryu as well as to people from other styles and other walks of life, I want to address this issue.

So here we go:

Not all karate is the same. There is a lot of poor-quality karate out there. If people went out in search of a martial art and looked at a karate place with poor quality, they might assume that all karate was like that. It isn't. But, like any stereotyped prejudice, it is not so easy to overcome a bad first impression. Especially when that impression is reinforced in their own mind by the art they took up. Many arts say "We are the best martial art. All other martial arts suck." This is not true. It can't be. Since they all say it, they can't all be right.

There is a wide variety of quality in any style. Most modern martial arts groups want to grow big. So, the standards drop and people get ranks and have some fun and whatever. Only a few very idealistic and strong people really plumb the depths of possibility in martial arts and approach the ideal and the potential that is available through martial practice. You can be among them.

Some styles may benefit from the reputation of one or a handful of great practitioners or founders. But they can't grow a big style holding every new member to the standard of that elite. Which is why martial arts trend up and then decline, and why sometimes they recover and return to their former glory.

Karate has risen and declined over the years, many times. Those changes have been based in the lives of the people who practiced it and the conditions of the societies and cultures in which they lived. But the name 'karate' didn't change. It was applied, in different times and different places, to very different arts.

Our style, Yamabayashi Ryu, Mountain Forest Style, is built on long-existing knowledge and techniques, transmitted from China and Japan as well as from Okinawa. It is unique in some ways. It may not resemble the karate people have encountered before – in strip malls and storefronts, Y's and campuses, rec centers, old mills, and schools around the world.

It has the fresh vitality of practical experience and deep traditional practice, built by hand, by dedicated people around the world, whose lives depend on getting it right.

It is not our role to criticize others. That brings no benefit. Let people enjoy their arts and their lives. But don't accept their criticism of some generic "karate" as accurate, as about us, or as reflecting at all on what we do.

Yamabayashi Ryu Dojo, carved by Tarleton Brooks

Empty Hand vs. Gun

When Hollywood hero Indiana Jones was threatened by a massive scimitar-wielding warrior he smirked, drew his pistol and shot the swordsman dead.

For some that incident put a bullet in the head of martial arts for practical self-defense. Done. Outdated. Silly. Gone the way of the cavalry charge, the knight in armor, the sword and shield.

That was the wrong conclusion.

Martial arts are practiced by every modern military. Insurgency and revolutionary groups do too. They post the video. They are not using martial arts as the primary way to fight their enemies. But they know the value of empty-hand training and skill. The US Army and the Marines have different empty-hand doctrines, but all personnel train in martial arts.

In a night club an unarmed man approached an active shooter from behind and threw him to the ground. The shooter dropped his rifle. The shooter reached for his pistol. The unarmed man, a retired Army officer, grabbed the pistol from the shooter's hand, used it as a club, subdued him, and held the shooter until help arrived.

On a train in France a US Airman, on vacation, saw a man enter the train with a rifle. Walking down the aisle, the man brought his rifle up to eye level, ready to shoot. While the terrified passengers ducked down behind the seats, the Airman got up, advanced on the gunman and grabbed the rifle. The shooter pulled the trigger. The rifle misfired. The shooter reached for his backup pistol, which also misfired. The airman seized it. Other passengers helped him to restrain the would-be assassin.

Another time not long ago a man walked in the front door of a busy café, drew a pistol and started shooting and killing the people sitting at the tables. The patrons dropped to the floor trying to hide until it was all over. In a few seconds the shooter's gun was empty, locked back. He reached into his jacket for another magazine. Most of the coffee drinkers remained frozen in place.

But two women at one of the tables understood what they were seeing. They knew they had seconds to act before the shooter could reload and start killing again. They rushed him, disarmed him, and with the help of some of the other people, held him.

Outcomes in a confrontation are not guaranteed. In each of those cases the empty-handed people prevailed over the assassins. In all cases the defenders were familiar with firearms; they understood the operation and the limitations of firearms. They also had martial skills and a martial mindset – to accept the risk, take the initiative, and go for it, until the threat was stopped.

In none of these cases did the unarmed people persist in their use of force beyond the moment when they were certain the threat was over.

Understanding arms-length empty-hand disarming techniques is useful. It may be that you are armed but do not have time to access your weapon, and may need to rely initially on an empty-hand response.

What is necessary in all of these situations is the self-confidence, skill, strength, and determination that come as a result of training in empty-hand self-defense with experience in responding to chaotic aggression. Not all martial arts know this. The military knows this. The paramilitaries know this. And we know it.

The same mindset applies in armed defense. Armed defense is used much more frequently against armed threats, and is much more reliable. But you know as well as I do, you do what you need to do, with what you have.

***

Three Instructor Stages

There are three levels of instructor in our style.

The first stage instructor demonstrates technical competence, and the interest and ability to share what they know with others.

The second stage instructor combines that with the ability to energize the practice of other people. That means to inspire them by example, encourage them individually and as a group, and lead the group to deeper competence.

The third stage instructor builds on that, using innovation and tradition, understanding this relationship as fruitful and as dangerous as the relationship between fire and water.

In cooking, fire and water have to be in balance. Too much fire and the food will burn. Too much water, the pot overflows, the fire goes out. When they work in harmony the food will be well-made: it will taste good and be nourishing.

That balance is critical for plants and animals and people – earth, water, light and heat have to be in balance. A flood, a drought, hail or frost, can ruin everything.

All instructors apply this balance – using the right amount of heat and pressure in each class to get good results from every student. Too much: people get hurt and discouraged. Too little: people stay unchallenged and complacent.

The third level instructor will apply this to the style as a whole, as well as to the training of individuals, to the design of the classes, and to the training methods.

Traditional transmission of knowledge and skill is done by example, in person – not mainly by books or records, or by theories, or by parables or stories, but by a live teacher in action, who embodies the skills and shares them.

The apprenticeship model is not limited to martial arts. It has been used to convey the methods of every traditional work skill and every life skill, from generation to generation. It remains the only way martial arts can be transmitted.

For traditional martial arts to fulfill their potential, and for us to fulfill ours, the balance between innovative vitality and adherence to tradition – the balance between fire and water – has to be precise.

***

Just, Not the Same

On the day I received these two belts they looked about the same. The same two-inch Shureido black belts, the same gold embroidered kanji, the same name, "Sakiyama Sogen," on one of the ends of each belt.

On the other end of the belts were two different phrases. One was **Ken Zen Ichi Nyo**, motto of Shoshin Nagamine, founder of Matsubayashi Shorin Ryu Karate. The other belt had **Oku Myo Zai Ren Shin** – the motto on the front wall of the dojo of Chojun Miyagi, Sakiyama Sogen's teacher, founder of Goju Ryu Karate.

I chose one of the belts to wear for dojo training. The other I put away for later, for the day when the first one would wear out. They don't look the same any more.

In the beginning practitioners are similar. All have a chance to learn and thrive. But not all do. Some strive. Some persist. Some move on. As beginners they were similar, after a while they become very different.

Ranking systems may or may not be just. But good training is. If you do the work, you get the results. If you don't, you don't. That is not subjective. It is fair.

***

Concealed in Kihon

Ikken hissatsu, 一拳必殺, may be an ideal way to resolve a lethal confrontation. There is a kind of myth-making about it. It seems simple. Why would you attempt anything else, if you were under a lethal threat. Some styles try to achieve this with ippon kumite, developing speed and precision. The phrase "ikken hissatsu" means one punch one kill. It is taken from traditional Japanese kenjitsu, sword fighting. In sword fighting it is meaningful.

We train to give full commitment to each technique. But ikken hissatsu is not always a reliable tactic for empty hand combatives. If the opponent has sound balance, has eyes on, and is attacking, then we will need to respond. Generally, our defense is designed as a multi-part sequence. None of the parts are "defensive" only.

The chudan uke, jodan uke and gedan uke, kihon or basic techniques which we learn on the first week of class – are called middle block, high block and down block in English.

Uke does not mean "block" in the sense of putting up a static obstacle, like the arms in the way of an incoming strike or grab. That type of protective covering is commonly used in boxing, where it is used against an opponent wearing heavy gloves, and where grappling is against the rules. It is not what we train to do in karate. The name of this class of techniques points to this insight. Uke, 受, means "receive", in the sense of receiving the incoming energy and will of an opponent. Chudan uke means receiving at mid-level. It does not mean a "chest block."

All three of these kihon techniques are the first two phases of multi-part responses to an incoming attack, which set up an ikken finishing technique.

To give an example: for the "middle block" the blocking arm crossing the body as you step forward intercepts the incoming punch and reroutes it past your body. That draws the attacker forward and places you inside his defensive range, and within reach of his targets.

Your same fist then returns across your body into position "in front of your shoulder." That move functions as a back fist to the jaw (possibly to the mental foramen, the carotid sinus, the mandibular angle, or any kyusho which is exposed by the initial contact when the attacker is drawn in). This will have a stunning effect, and disrupt his body architecture and balance.

A third component of the "kihon" tactic is a reverse punch or other follow-up hand or foot technique which, when used against an off-balance, destabilized and stunned attacker, completes the series and may resolve the encounter.

If it doesn't, you continue, just as we do in all our kata.

These three uke techniques can be applied individually but are segments of a continuum of movement, that protects everywhere, up and down the center line of the body, and continues, to power the counterattack. They appear in kata this way frequently, as in the fourth to fifth direction and seventh to eighth direction in our first kata, Fukyugata ichi.

That is the fundamental kihon "defensive" sequence. Launched with good speed, power and focus, using your whole body, good foundation, waist rotation, rerouting and neutralizing the opponent's power, this represents a basic tactical approach that we learn from day one, beginning with our kihon techniques and first kata.

***

Resistance is Futile

Speed is critical. We are not born with a predetermined ability to move quickly. Like power, endurance, flexibility, focus, skills and tactics, we train it to improve it.

To increase speed, we create conditions in the dojo where speed is essential: kumite is one way, speed drills on targets are another, two-person contact drills, with accelerating pace, are others. As we practice this way we build the fast-twitch cells of our muscles which make us fast.

We can also do speed work in kata. Using kata, kihon and other solo drills – when we are focused on our own body – we can focus on speed.

In addition to developing fast-twitch muscles there is a second way to increase speed: detect and remove the physical habits which are obstacles to speed.

Eliminate Resistance in Opposing Muscles

One way to do this is to eliminate tension in opposing muscles. Each of our arms and legs have muscles that extend the limb – the extensors – and another that pull it back – the flexors. The tension we unconsciously hold in the muscles slows down our punches, kicks or other techniques. As we train, we mentally scan the body for tension, detect it, and learn to release it.

Staying loose when executing a whipping, ballistic punch or kick – with no tension in the flexors until the instant of impact, and then snapping it back with no residual tension in the extensors – increases the speed and multiplies the power of the technique.

To make that a habit, and to avoid tension creeping back into the muscles while you are continuing to practice, it is good to take a long enough pause between the moves to mentally scan for tension and then release it. As you get used to moving without holding tension, you can speed up the sequences of techniques, and not tighten up again.

Eliminate Resistance in Body Architecture

We also might hold tension in the core, back, shoulders, lats and traps. It's good to check to see if you your shoulders are rising up as you make effort. This will reduce the speed, power and stability of your arm techniques, so it is good to get your shoulders relaxed and low.

Another place to look for tension is in the lower abdomen, at the hara. People hold tension there because it feels strong, or because they are pulling their stomach in, and it becomes a habit. Tension held there distorts the axis of the spine. If the spine is not tall and vertical, we will lean away from the central axis of motion. That adds extra effort, as our muscles work hard to keep us upright, creating stiffness in the movement. It also off-balances the body, whether still or moving, because the spine is canted forward when stationary, and off-axis – that is out of alignment with the center of gravity – when moving and turning.

With good vertical posture this habit of resilience instead of tension is easy to build. It is essential for generating power and for maintaining effortless balance. We can easily train them in kata and kumite, and then transfer these skills into kumite, partner drills, or whatever we are doing. When the body is loose until the instant of impact, we maximize speed using ballistic technique, instead of relying on linear thrust or leverage.

Mass x Acceleration = Force

For generating force, acceleration is the variable we can control. The mass of our fist or foot or arm or leg is pretty much fixed. Although there are many factors that contribute to speed and to the effectiveness of our techniques – building fast-twitch muscle and eliminating resistance and tension in the body are keys to increasing acceleration.

People sometimes hold tension in the body because subjectively it "feels" strong. There is definitely a time to be tense – at the point of contact of a technique, or in naihanchi kata for example. But for most techniques, eliminating resistance is necessary.

***

No Menkyo Kaiden for You!

Fixed and bounded systems can be fully known. In martial arts this provides a convenient and reassuring way of thinking about the content of styles. But it is a fiction. To be sure there needs to be a clear, well-defined, structured knowledge base. It needs to be scrupulously acquired and mastered.

But this should be understood as the platform for exploration, development and innovation, not the end of the road.

The familiar Shu Ha Ri 守破離 "Protect, Break, Depart" formula arises from this insight. It is not mystical or esoteric. It is mature, confident and honest.

There can never be "total transmission", in a sense. Of course, a teacher can approve a disciple's competence in a set of techniques, and certify his or her authority to teach the system. But the system is the teacher's system. He formed it or learned it under particular conditions: the demands of his life, his culture, his environment and his training. Detached from the conditions that engendered it the system becomes isolated and begins to decompose. Unless new life is introduced into it, with fresh demands, including purposeful engagement with unpredictable conditions, the system will stiffen, wither and die. The master's experience was his. You can benefit from it. But you can't have it. Your experience needs to be yours.

Menkyo 免許 is a license. Kaiden 皆伝 is a total transmission, or a formal initiation into an art.

The Menkyo Kaiden, handed from a teacher to a student, may be a personal matter between the two of them. It may have significance within a group of practitioners: as a transfer of institutional authority, defining a requisite scope of knowledge and skill. It may mark the passing of the torch to the next generation. From time to time, it functioned as a professional license – authenticating a person's claim of skill, and, by restricting entry into the field, limiting competition, and enhancing prestige. It may express the tradition of veneration of ancestors which privileges the continuity of generations as a source of stability, legitimacy and prestige.

But however well it may be used, in reality, even if you are approved to teach your teacher's entire system, you are not finished.

You cannot stop exploring, learning, testing, – at once humbly and energetically – discovering new depth, new subtlety, new dimensions, new connections – if your practice is alive, and if your life is on the line.

Can you pass it all on? To another person who has a different life, different experience, different aspirations? You can show them the foundation. You can model the approach. Then they are on their own. That is the Ri 離 in "Shu Ha Ri" 守破離.

Any body of knowledge, identified, codified and mastered is inherently incomplete. It may work extremely well. It may be formidable, awesome, stunning in its power. But still, it came into existence in time, space and mind, based on experience, perspectives and objectives which are particular.

The relationship between maintaining patterns of training in a defined curriculum on the one hand and a willingness to examine, explore, refine and deepen on the other, is similar to the relationship between fire and water.

If fire and water meet by chance, they will try to destroy each other. In harmony they sustain life.

Without a well-formed system there is no way to forge skill and spirit – newcomers would lose their way trying to cut a fresh path, unguided, through the infinite possibilities. Without the freedom to test, refine and re-engineer the old ways just get old. Once-great achievements become museum pieces, as decontextualized and dry as a mounted shako or a dusty pickelhaube.

But with freedom, based on real skill-mastery, wisely applied in training and in combatives, the hearts and minds of practitioners come to life.

To achieve high skill takes more than rote repetition, but continual exploration and refinement are no guarantee either. Those can go on forever and lead nowhere. It takes certainty about what matters and what problems we need to solve.

**

Dō as Jitsu

Sakiyama Sogen

Dō 道 arises on the basis of jitsu 術. Do and jitsu are not separate or alternative paths. They are one. By doing the hard work needed for technical mastery, disciplining the mind, strengthening the will, overcoming obstructions to the skillful use of the body – all required for karate jitsu – we move along the path of karate-do.

People feel lonely. Choices seem pointless. People feel depressed, anxious, bored, resentful and frustrated. Aggression erupts. The prescribed remedies: drugs and alcohol, porn and promiscuity, wealth and power, pleasure and leisure, offer relief quickly followed by agitation, yearning and nothing. Lives stop, spin and come apart.

Cultural conditions are undermining loving families, the value of work, orientation in the transcendent. What do practitioners do about that?

We get together with mutual respect and shared aspiration. We learn, sweat, live and train together. We challenge each other. We appreciate each other. We act with purpose: To unify our bodies and our minds, and make them our own. To take command of our conditions, make choices, increase our ability to take care of ourselves and look out for others. We choose the deep, demanding heat and pressure of training in which the possibility of success and failure are always with us. At the end of a session of training, at the end of a life of training, we feel the release, elevation, and peace that come from doing honest, hard work.

Training once in a while will not have much effect. Making it a lifelong habit will have a transformative effect that never ends. Who knows what challenges we will face: Threats. Disrespect. Deception. Assaults to reason and dignity, to friends and family, to body and mind. We prepare to prevail. We live with honor. We go deeply into this world as we go beyond it.

Demanding, honest training is medicine. It is a refuge from cultural dissolution. It is a path to freedom and dignity. That is how jitsu becomes dō and dō becomes jitsu.

(1973 Photo credit Hick Ngow Lee)

***

Play, Work, War

As our lives are increasingly isolated and atomized, we begin to take for granted that the best advice available will come from media personalities and their apps. The clever ones know what sells. So, it is no surprise that so much of the physical training advice and meditation advice coming our way promote continual self-regard.

Presentations focused on "my body··· my stats··· my routine··· my supplements··· my schedule··· my performance···" get our attention. All that lonely self-regard produces anxiety. It craves acknowledgment. It derives validity from record keeping. Even in something as unworldly as meditation, the trending apps and websites from high profile advisors with millions of followers, even the ones who are teaching you that you don't have a self, foster self-centeredness – "my practice··· my tradition··· my experience··· my teacher··· my view··· my samadhi··· my nirvana··· my etc."

We aspire. Self-centeredness is an obstacle. It replaces enjoyment, challenge and purpose. It prevents mastery. There is another way to consider.

Good physical training and mind training, include aspects of play, work and war. Traditional approaches to training include these three. Modern, high-tech, solitary training is deficient in some or all of them. Play, work and war are communal, purposeful and urgent. Martial arts and meditation were both created to address matters of life and death.

Kids play hide and seek. Hide and seek is modeled on predator and prey. For millions of years, it was handy to be good at hiding when a predator was nearby, and to hunt successfully, when prey was nearby. These drives and skills are deeply rooted in us. People who got good at them got to live.

Kids love to play hide and seek. They get the game right away. Hide and seek is a thrill when they win, and even when they lose.

In traditional societies sports were war training. Sometimes they were also work training.

Settled people needed to protect themselves from raiders. And raiders needed to train to overwhelm and rob settled people. Both settlers and raiders quickly discovered that "just doing it" was not a reliable a path to victory. Training improved your chances. And training hard improved them more.

Long jump, high jump, sprint, distance run, hammer throw, caber toss, climbing, single contests, team sports, stick sports, ball sports, from native American stone-ball games to the Athenian Olympics, in every country, in every traditional culture, from polis to village, people played - because it was fun, and because it kept them sharp and in shape so they could stay alive under pressure.

Athletics helped create defined and stable dominance hierarchies and mating status, which create order and let people put their attention on other matters, at least temporarily.

Rams, for example, don't kill each other in mating competition, they smash horns and the winner gets to mate. The other one eats some grass and tries again next week. Herds would not have survived eons of predatory pursuits if the males in the herd all killed each other in rutting season. They worked out a better way. So have we. And everyone who participates gets stronger, healthier and more deeply embedded in the group.

People train and compete in war, mating and work. Dragon boat races in Okinawa are an example of community competition in nautical skills which, in the pre-modern days, everyone needed to keep sharp, all year round.

In the Okinawan tug of war thousands of people pull a 1000' foot long, six-foot-thick rope, made by hand by all the people in all the villages, kept people working together, and competing in skills on which their lives and livelihoods depended, all year round. Making nets and ropes, being able to pull rigging lines on ships in a gale, were critical life skills. They worked, they played, they competed. Some won some lost. Everyone benefitted.

Photo credit Stripes.com

Martial arts were also practiced all year round, in the villages and cities, for health and fitness, for confidence, focus and defense, and because each person was a member of their community, and that's what people did.

The primary focus was not on ones' self. The primary focus was not on "my biceps, my heart rate, my blood oxygenation, or my split times." That may be part of the mix. But attention on other people, the life of the village, the work to be done, the life to be shared, the people to be defended, all played a role in the motivations and objectives of everyone's training and practice.

This perspective plays a central role in our practice today. Working together for a common purpose, is more fun, more satisfying, and yields higher performance for a lifetime than vanity. You wouldn't think you would have to point this out. But you do.

***

P

Penetrating the Truth

When you begin training you get advice. You try to understand. Sometimes the advice is easy to use, like "Close your fist." Often, even though the words are familiar and the grammar makes sense, what to do with the advice remains obscure. Then later, as a result of practice, the meaning becomes clear. Then, when the time is right, the same few words of advice can change everything.

Here is an example:

腰如轴立，手似轮行

Yang Jwing-ming's translation:

The waist firm like an axle, the hands move like wheels

(From his book Emei Baguazhang.)

Andrea Falk's translation, appearing along with the original Chinese at *DiGuoWong*:

The waist is like an axle, the hands turn like wheels

This advice is perfectly accurate. That is what we do and how it works. We probably wouldn't think of it on our own. We probably wouldn't move this way if it wasn't pointed out. But after it is, we can use it to make the most of the power, range and speed of our whole body.

The character 腰, used in the above Chinese quotation, is pronounced "koshi" in Japanese. In some training "the koshi" is treated as something mysterious, elusive, hard to describe, harder to comprehend.

But "koshi" is just a normal word. The mystification disappears as you use the advice: awareness of your waist in motion, connecting its motion down to your hips and lower back, up to your spine, out through your arms and, into your technique, creating a habit of moving with the whole body, generating motion in the limbs by means of rotation at the waist. If you have not practiced much, this may be mysterious. If you have practiced for a while, it is obvious. Same body. Same principle. Same words. Different understanding as a result of practice.

There are endless pieces of advice like this which are shared in the course of training. The words become useful as we move. As we explore the meaning of the advice, we use it to explore the purpose of our technique.

We may also discover that much of the advice we are learning is universal, not limited in application to one martial art, or even to martial arts in general. The approach to movement in Chinese internal and external martial arts are different. Differences in tactics and techniques are evident in the Okinawan martial arts as well: Shorin, Goju and Uechi are not the same. But many of the training principles are. Marketing and mythology notwithstanding, individual martial arts are not completely separate, different or opposed.

I cited the above example about the waist because although at first it sounds mystical, it is natural. It applies to baseball, tennis, swimming and golf, among others, and is commonly used in coaching these sports at the competitive level. The language is different but the principle is the same.

In many ways all human bodies work alike. Despite our differences, our minds are susceptible to the same healthy and unhealthy influences. Accepting the limits of our bodies at the beginning of practice as "the way I am" is an error. We can change the way we are.

Damatte keiko is good advice. "Shut up and train." It is a terse antidote for over-explaining. But wait - it is conveyed in words. If you take it literally, you would never say it. A few well-chosen words, at the right time, to the right person can change everything. It can be like daybreak. Or a shock.

***

Breaking Good

Once your opponent's balance is broken you can neutralize his threat.

He may break his own balance by error or lack of skill. Or you can break it for him, by guile or contact. Our own balance will be attacked. We cannot afford to lose it. We need to maintain it or to recover right away.

We have control over what we do – how we fight, how we train and how we live. We may have the chance to take control over our opponent's balance. We will be prepared to exploit that moment only by mastering our own balance, continually.

Which is why trained people are different from untrained people. We perform differently under pressure. And we behave differently when there is no pressure.

But to have this advantage, you have to dig deep into training. It is not convenient and it is not easy.

The instantaneous reversals of technique and maneuver we use to outperform an opponent – even someone larger, stronger or out of their mind – are the result of long, hard training. You cannot just learn them and do them. It will not work, no matter how talented an athlete you are.

Entry into deep states of flow, which we depend upon for both instantaneous and sustained high performance, and to reach the gateway of insight, are not achievable without extensive training.

We cannot practice occasionally. A three-times a week training schedule is minimum for high performance results. It is not a minimum for fun, interesting activity, self-defense skill acquisition and a good whole-body workout. It is a minimum for deep, transformative practice. It is not for everyone.

To sustain high output and high awareness over the whole class or over many classes, year after year, even when you are tired, even when you are sore, even when you are busy and under pressure from life demands outside the dojo, is unusual. It is necessary to set them aside and do deep training, continually, over an extended period for true transformation to happen.

Vacations, travel, work, family time, special events, illness, injury, friends, distractions, shocks and surprises, are all a part of life. And training continues. If you miss a class, you do an individual workout. If you get hurt, you work around the injury. If you are busy, you step out of the office for five minutes and do five slow motion kata, and then get back to it, refreshed and more productive.

You balance urgency with patience, you keep your balance, and let nothing stand in your way.

***

Empty Hand vs. Drugs

Training as we do is the opposite of addiction.

We move forward, like a river. We continue, following our course, with purpose. We change. We meet obstacles, we adapt, we continue. Sometimes the way is smooth and then it narrows, we hit cascades, whitewater. We deal with it. We continue. Our life has direction. If we train well, it may be that whoever we meet can draw something good from us, as we can from them.

Addicts don't live this way. They don't flow on. They remain caught in a cycle, a whirlpool of desire and gratification, looped endlessly. Their first taste of pleasure is never duplicated, but they pursue it, endlessly. Their pleasure recedes, replaced by even more urgent desire. Their desire is obstructed – they have no dope. Fever, panic and frenzy set in. Instead of flowing on through life the addict gets stuck in place, like a whirlpool caught at the edge of a rock in a river, revolving faster and faster, deeper and deeper, pulling whatever is near it into itself, as desire turns toward gratification which turns back into craving, turning around again and again in an intensifying loop of mind and action, with no way out.

Drugs and alcohol are obvious addictions. Promiscuity, craving for wealth, status, indolence and attention all work the same way. Addicts become slaves of their dealers. They hand over everything: first their attention, then their wealth, then their time. They devour their relationships, ruining their bodies, numbing and coarsening their hearts and minds, robbing their neighbors, anyone who comes close, anyone they can get to, as the vortex of their addiction spins faster and faster, out of control, controlling them, eating them alive.

What we do in our training is the opposite of addiction. We live with purpose. We take care of ourselves and other people. We value our bodies and minds and keep them healthy, so we can use them to bring benefit to ourselves and to our friends and families. To do good work, as we make our way.

We might think of addicts as the people we see nodding, mewling and puking on the street: crazy, needy, violent, pathetic, menacing or smelly. But some addicts are well-dressed, well-informed and powerful. Drawing the whole world into the vortex of their desire; the whole world invited to witness and admire them, to reflect back to them their authority, status and fame.

They are just as desperate as the addicts sleeping on the sidewalk, as blind, as obsessed with the next hit – the next deal, the next payoff, the next movie, the next meeting, the next sex contact, the next sugar rush, the next assertion of power that reminds them and others of their dominance, the extent of their influence.

They cannot escape the prison of their own minds, no matter how far their jet flies, how exquisite their destination, how notable their friends. The jolt of gratification quickly passes. Then disturbance, fever and panic follow. They need more, different, better, faster. Seething, strategizing, anxiety, pleasure and gloating preoccupy them, and destroy the hope of happiness, peace and satisfaction which they crave. They cannot flow on. They turn and spin, again and again, in place, trapped until they are torn apart by the maelstrom, caught in a vortex of clueless desire, gratification and pain, repeated endlessly.

Addiction spins down. And it will draw in whatever is nearby. Training with purpose, flows on and on in freedom. It changes. It adapts. It nourishes life, nearby and far away. Our horizon opens out. Wide as the mountain sky. Endless as the widest river, on and on it goes before us, and we are welcome.

***

Sweet Dreams

In the time of decline and dissolution people will eat food which does not nourish…
    -Bhagavad Gita, SB1.4.17-18

Sugar is an addictive drug. It makes you fat, sick and depressed. It has many forms and names. It is in most manufactured food. Addiction to it sets in rapidly. It is difficult to quit. But once you do quit it is easy to do without. And when you do without it you can do better at everything you do.

It is addictive in two ways.

It effects brain chemistry. You feel happy when you anticipate eating some. But that happiness wears off. Then you crave more, so you don't start to feel flat or sad. You become dependent on sugar. But sugar does not make you happy.

It effects blood chemistry too. Your insulin level surges to metabolize it. Sugar makes you crave more sugar. You always feel hunger. That's not normal. That's addiction.

Any addiction is a big ball and chain. You drag it around with you wherever you go. It's always there, demanding your attention. All addicts experience this. They crave their dope – whatever they are addicted to – they always want some. Including sugar.

It effects all their relationships. Little by little all they can really focus on, all they really care about, is feeding their addiction. People, responsibility, work, the joys of life and the world around them, all fade. Only their dope stands out as sharp and meaningful and real.

If you should stand between an addict and their drug, even with good information, the best of intentions, with kind and caring words, even with love in your heart, they will ignore you or evade you.

If they can't, they will get angry with you. They will see you as an obstacle to their happiness. As someone who is attempting to hurt them. As someone who is trying to take their freedom. They will try to eliminate your influence. Or they may try to eliminate you. Can sugar be that bad?

Drug dealers, on the corner, in the store, or on the screen, are not your friends. They may seem nice. But they are not looking out for you. They may say they sell what they sell to survive.

They may say that if they didn't sell it to you, somebody else would. They may say what you do with what they sell is your business, not theirs. They may say they knew not what they did. Or that they didn't know how much you would use.

Whatever the merits of those arguments, they are not looking out for you. Even if they know you well. Someone who provides good, nutritious food, with love in it, is looking out for you. Even if they have never met you.

To excel in training, we are concerned with output – with our performance. We will be scrupulous about how we move, how often we train, how precise our technique, how hard we work, how completely we dedicate ourselves to our art and to each moment of practice – measuring our performance against that of our training partners, competitors, aggressors, and ourselves – as we advance.

To excel in our training, we also should be concerned with input: what ideas we welcome, what techniques we choose to study, who we choose to spend time with, whose influence we accept, how we educate and nourish our minds – and also how we fuel and nourish our bodies.

We would not willingly take poison. We avoid toxic people, toxic ideas, toxic environments. We can choose healthy inputs which will support and further our training – in making our body strong, flexible, and fast, and in keeping our minds clear, sharp and skilled.

It takes a few weeks to break sugar addiction. After that there is no issue. A difficulty is that sugar addiction is acceptable. It appears innocent. As if it was harmless, pleasant and under control. For most people it is none of those.

There are people in offices, cubicles, conference rooms and at screens around the world deciding how many hundreds of millions of dollars to spend on marketing and advertising exciting new colorful, flavorful, caffeinated drinks. Nice looking, successful and happy people, well-lit and expertly photographed, will make it look good. It is entirely possible that not one of those people, in the conference rooms, in the commercials, thought to ask "Is this good for anyone?"

They calculated the ROI and gave it the green light.

It is common for people to make themselves sick by conforming to cultural conventions that seem normal. By adapting to a pathological environment, they become unhealthy. They are enabled by people who do not care for them.

We are not victims by nature. It is our responsibility to take care of ourselves. Physical self-defense is important. Self-defense goes beyond combatives.

***

The Moment of Truth

If we allow our lives to be framed by the choice between gain and loss, fame and obscurity, praise and blame, and pleasure and pain then we are done. It is too late.

As practitioners we have a better basis for deciding what to do and what to avoid.

By practitioners I do not mean all people who do martial arts. I mean people who are serious about it. How do we decide what to do and what to avoid? What on earth would make more sense than choosing between easy or hard, gain or loss, fame or obscurity, praise or blame, pleasure or pain? What else is there?

Those are the choices that guide the world. Hollywood, Washington and Wall Street live by them. Empires and animals do the best they can with them. Moths, circling the flame, wondering what's burning, are trying to do something fun.

Those are not the choices that practitioners need to use.

The alternative to pursuing gain, pleasure, fame, and praise, while doing everything to avoid loss, pain, obscurity and blame is making your first concern the choice between right and wrong. It is not hard to understand. It is urgent.

And it is not all relative: Don't kill people. Don't lie to them. Don't steal their stuff. Don't misuse sex. Don't drink or do drugs. Don't bad-mouth people. Don't curse people. Don't talk unless you mean it and it is useful. Don't crave what other people have. Don't tolerate hatred or ill will in your heart. Devote yourself to practice, and penetrate to the heart of the truth.

That is how to be strong.

In the midst of madness, violence, seduction and chaos, this choice makes life worthy and good. It is difficult and now as always, it is dangerous. You would think I wouldn't need to put these obvious encouragements in a book about training. There are plenty of good people trying to do the right thing. But they are under a lot of pressure.

***

The Momentum of Truth

At first enthusiasm gets you in the door. You imagine yourself as you want to be, with great skill, great confidence, great power. The reality of the first, hard steps in training is acceptable. You can overlook not knowing what you are doing, not being able to do as much as you want, being lower in rank and status than other people who have been around for a while. It is acceptable, because you have a dream of who you want to be, and you feel you have found a way to get there.

That changes. The excitement of the dream fades in light of the reality of the demands of daily training. As if someone had flipped on the lights in a room while you were watching a movie.

The realistic world on the screen fades in the light, the illusion ends. The chairs and the floor and the walls of the room, a little worn, the flat, mundane features of the world, impinge on your sense as the wonderful enchantment of the film vaporizes.

Then where are you? In training, at this stage, you are face to face with yourself. That's you in the mirror, not as you want to be but as you are. The work of transformation is difficult. The results come slowly. Sometimes they are invisible. The difficulty however is quite apparent. The sore muscles. The demands on your vacillating focus. The trial and error, and trying again. The interesting, pleasurable, relaxing and easy things you could be doing if you were somewhere else.

But then, you have put a lot into it. And when you think about it, you get a lot out of it. You know that once you get in the door, and change into your gi, and start to move, it is a good thing, it is your art, it is your process and it is working. You are getting it. You are getting good. You are looking good too. People notice it. People say so.

You know that once you change back into your regular clothes and head back out onto the street, the world seems more beautiful, more at peace and more yours than it did when you walked into the dojo, after a hard day of work, a long day at school, a busy day filled with family responsibilities and the demands of daily life.

You enjoy that moment, out there in the night air, breathe deep and keep on, recommitting yourself to the difficult, demanding process, and you go home and get some rest.

You notice that the people who have been at it for a long time seem good. Not perfect; but you can see the accumulation of the years of their effort in their skill, their poise and their concern for the people around them. You can see that their training has a momentum that carries them forward into the next posture, the next move, the next class, the next day, and on and on. Not falling. Not pushing. Just the calm, energized momentum of a skilled practitioner, a skillful life, a life of practice, of life in action.

You notice the ones who fell by the wayside. People you started with who disappeared. Maybe you run into one or two around town or in the park, at the store or at school and you see how they are doing. Maybe the direction of their life has some momentum too. Maybe they are at ease and happy and found other things they like to do. They are focused on their family, their work, and this is the time of life for that. And they tell you they are looking forward to getting back to training soon, when they can.

Or maybe the momentum of their lives is carrying them down, not up. Maybe the accumulation of small choices is burdening them. Maybe they are occupied with trivia and harmful things. They are in a dark frame of mind, frustrated and searching, not at peace, and not focused on a direction, and yet the momentum of their choices carries them, and accelerates, until the choices they make aren't really theirs, until they aren't really choices at all.

The accumulation of small effects, good or bad, creates a pattern of life, a path of life, a life. At first, we do not notice it. But soon it is unmistakable. Seeing only what is near we miss what is far off. What is possible. Who we can be. What we can do.

***

The Benevolence of the Butcher

"It is not from the benevolence of the butcher, the brewer, or the baker, that we expect our dinner, but from their regard to their own interest."

-Adam Smith, 1776, <u>An Inquiry into the Nature and Sources of the Wealth of Nations</u>

Adam Smith was describing how free markets work. No one knows everything. But each individual can make calculations based on what they do know.

Those individual choices make markets work efficiently. Adam Smith recognized that individual self-interest can optimize personal satisfaction and social well-being.

We can see a corollary of this principle in the dojo. Each person is there because it benefits them to be there. By pursuing their own aims each member furthers the objectives of everyone else there. There will be competition. There will be inequality of ability, effort and reward. But everyone in the room can benefit from the heat and pressure of training in the company of like-minded people. Everyone benefits from the skill, determination and vitality of everyone around them.

But in that corollary, we can spot the unexpressed proviso in Adam Smith's famous quote. Because in the dojo, whether we are butcher, brewer, baker or otherwise, we all depend on one another's benevolence. Not in the sense that everyone should be pleasant. Not in the sense that we are acting somehow against our own interests to altruistically prioritize the interests of the others.

But in the sense that we all know the rules of the dojo and tacitly or expressly agree to conform to them. In dojo training we stop a technique before it will cause injury.

We follow the instructor's directions. We enter on time and leave when finished.

With all the rules of conduct and decorum, stated and inferred, each of us follows the procedures, techniques, training methods, customs, language, roles and the cultural framework which makes training harmonious, orderly and productive for all of us.

If those rules are set aside, there is no more training, and no more development. If people attacked each other at will, if people ignored instructions, if passivity, brutality and hard work were equally okay, there would be nothing for anyone.

In this way we depend on the benevolence of even our rivals and adversaries, our most challenging training partners: we can trust their willingness to follow the rules of the game. Their self-control makes it possible for all of us to make the most of our training.

If the butcher, the brewer or the baker used threats and lies to further their interests the market would cease to exist. If they used conspiracy, deception and force – what gangs, raiders and hegemons all use to get their way – market intelligence would be irrelevant. Everyone becomes needy and fearful. For a functioning society we do depend on the benevolence of the butcher, the brewer and the baker, in this sense.

To work well, social structures, including markets and dojos, require respect for other people.

Efficient and benevolent social relations require us to honor our word and to accept the conventions of morality – whether motivated by the prospect of embarrassment by being exposed for a breach of trust, the fear of being found guilty of a violation of law, or restrained by our own virtue, persuaded of the happiness of others and the rewards of decency in this life and the next.

These factors promote the benevolence of all parties in the group – in the dojo or the market – even as we all pursue our own interests.

Without the rules, we have chaos. Then instead of creating value, value drains away. Instead of increasing our skill and strength, they erode. Instead of order and the pursuit of happiness we have decline, abuse and despair. No matter how hard we push each other, how tough, strong, skilled, dedicated and clever we are, we all depend to some degree on the benevolence of one another for the success of our society.

This is not something that can be taken for granted. As martial artists we use these values in the dojo. If we can inspire this and apply this in the wider world, that is a good result of dojo practice. In this sense we do depend on the benevolence of the butcher. When we cannot there is trouble.

***

Kansha

Here's why we have the Gratitude calligraphy in front of the dojo: Gratitude is not a mushy, sentimental feeling. It is a hard practice. It's up there as a reminder to appreciate having a good place to train, and to appreciate each other.

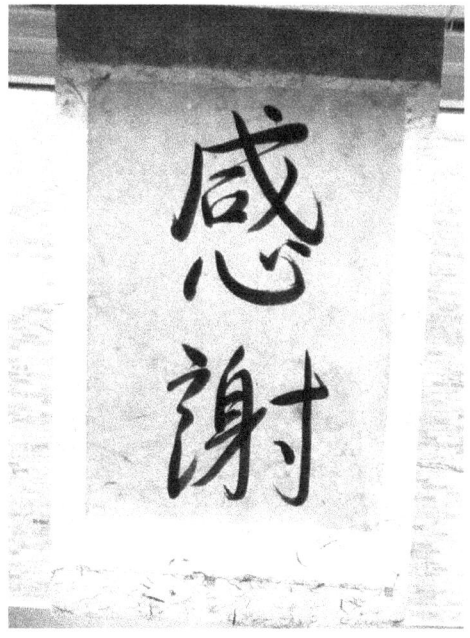

"Kansha"

shodo by Chie Nakata

It's easy to focus on what's lacking. Faults of the space, limitations of the schedule, shortcomings of people, our own defects and limitations, an unknown imaginary something else out there that might be better, or more, or different. Those pre-occupations are obstacles to training, as they are to friendship, family, and achievement. They are countered by gratitude.

Are we thankful for everything? Do we ignore flaws? Do we stop seeking, exploring, questioning and testing? No.

Are we thankful for pain, injury, irritating people, the limits of our bodies, our minds, our schedules, our lifetimes? Not in some tolerant, sentimental, make-believe way. Not by sighing or shrugging or saying "So it goes."

The relevant guidance is this:

In the hands of a master nothing is wasted.

In the woodworker's shop next to our old dojo wood scraps get saved and even the saw dust had its uses. People who hunted to live found a use for everything: meat, sinews, bones, hides, organs. Nothing was wasted. What they had was hard to get. They were grateful when they got it.

Our time and training are just as valuable. Just as urgent. Just as hard to get. Every class, every technique, everyone we train with, counts. If we appreciate what we have, we can make the most of it. When obstacles arise, we can use them.

We may be free to waste time, and even to kill time. But for a real practitioner there are no extra moments. Most of us cannot use everything skillfully. But to have this as an ideal, to use it in training, like having an ideal posture to strive for in kata, takes us further than we could go without it.

The language of scorn, irony, cynicism and mockery is common currency. A mindset of appreciation and respect is not.

To value what we have, to take care of it, to appreciate the people we share it with, is worth cultivating.

We cultivate power in training. To endure power depends on right and justice. Otherwise, power is trivial. It will be like a straw fire: hot, bright, gone.

We did not invent our bodies, our minds, the language we use, the buildings we live in, the food we eat, or the kata we use to train. It is useful to notice that. Lots of what we have came to us through the efforts of people we will never know. What will we do with what we have? In what condition will we pass it on?

That is why "Gratitude" is up there in the front window of the dojo.

***

Defense Against Violence and Decadence

You might never get mugged or even confronted. But our bodies and minds are under threat. Family life and personal relationships are under attack. Health and vitality arc under attack. Work and property are under attack. Religious and spiritual life are under attack. Personal worth is devalued and dignity is degraded.

We can defend against these threats.

Some approaches to martial arts are trivial. Some are unhealthy. Some are lame, expensive and over-hyped. Some think all martial arts is like that. An old instructor used to say, after class "Hey, It's all showbiz!" Maybe he was. But it isn't.

***

The Fog of Peace

We learned during the lockdown. We may draw on those lessons again:

Modern military commanders can map and model a vast battlespace and watch it change in real time. They can locate fighters and civilians, guns and armor, aircraft and satellites, threats and targets, caches and fortification, comms, changes of posture and subtle movements that signal a new phase is imminent. They can act on that intelligence to their advantage. Theoretically.

There is always uncertainty. Von Clausewitz was concerned with "friction." That was his word for the inconsistencies in planning and execution, errors in communication, judgement, intelligence, the breakdown in command, supply and on-the-ground capability, the enemy's deception, unknown strengths and vulnerabilities, plans, alliances and resources. This uncertainty is the "fog of war." It is relevant to every fighter.

In a crisis we detect threats. We spot opportunities. We feel compelled to act. The situation is abnormal. It feels about to shift. We have not seen something just like this before. Maybe a great transformation is underway.

What do we do? Our information is imperfect. Successful commanders and fighters do not overcome this fog. They do not magically see through it. They act within it based on what they know, intuit and want.

In the heat of confrontation or competition martial artists are trained to act with incomplete information. It is not that the shadows disappear. They do not rule. Our training and experience kick in.

Our current world situation does not appear to be what we trained for. For a moment at least, it seems we are operating in the fog of peace. After decades of daily classes, dojos are closed. We are training remotely or in pairs.

There is a lot of new silence. Roads were busy. Now a passing delivery truck or police cruiser gets a look. We're in the flight path of the airport. Planes were overhead all the time. No more.

We hear the birds. But we don't hear the sounds of co-workers, classrooms, meetings, sports, friends out for the evening. We don't hear the familiar dojo sounds of counting, kata, commands and kiai. It's silent. But even now, it is easy to get confused by all the noise. The signals are confusing.

Crossing paths with strangers at the post office or the store a month ago was anonymous. Then for a week or two strangers connected with shared interest. Now it's changed again, to furtive, to a dread of everyone and everything. As if eye contact could spread cooties. As if hurry could keep the invisible enemy from your throat.

I spent years as a detective. I investigated robberies, assaults, rapes, murders and fraud. I spoke to lots of witnesses, victims, and suspects. Some people lied to me. Some told the truth. Some tried a clever combination of the two.

There are things that liars do that give them away. They can't help doing it. It's no secret.

A sign that someone may be lying is instead of informing you they try to persuade you. They insist, they emote, they repeat, they plead, they change details in the middle of the story for effect, they embellish, they accuse, they swear to God. That's not definitive. But it's a clue. You need to look closer.

We try to rely on the media for information, to orient and to decide what to do. We need to look closer. We have a hunch the fog of peace is unlikely to lift right away. We will have to investigate deeply enough to act, but not so much that we allow our opportunity to act slip by.

We are practitioners. Our field of action is training, persistently and sincerely. If we are displaced by circumstances we adapt and continue. We may not have complete knowledge of the space we are in or the way events will unfold. We may not have an optimal path. But we can act. We can train. We can connect with one another.

The production company that made the Ninja Turtle comics and movies had their studios next to our dojo, long ago. They were very serious and funny people. Amidst all their well-recognized creativity I thought they had an underappreciated idea that I really liked. Practitioners really are like turtles, in a way. Turtles have a place to stay wherever they go. When they get tired, they pull in their legs and go to sleep. Then they wake up, stick their legs back out, and get on with it. No problem. Practitioners carry a dojo with them wherever they go. We wake up and get on with it. No problem.

We may not be able to see through the fog our world is in right now. We may not be able to get reliable intelligence that will allow us to map our action space, or life space, or anticipate every emerging threat or opportunity. We can persist in training with energy and sincerity. No need to let the fog obscure our purpose or plan of action. We continue to strengthen our mind and body, refine our lives, and do what we can for the people around us.

This fog is not an obstacle. Our way ahead is clear.

***

Appendix One
Zen Doctrines of Enlightenment

Notes on the Heart Sutra

Below are versions of the Heart Sutra in Japanese romaji and English. Take a look at the use of the negation "Mu" which is translated as "No." Insight into the significance of mu, as presented in this sutra, for adherents of this tradition, is central to liberation, the highest and final goal of the tradition.

The premise is our misunderstanding of the way things exist leads to negative emotions and harmful actions which are the cause of suffering.

In the section on Joshu's Mu, the story of the Diamond Sutra master and of Mumon, in the sphere of Zen practice, and of Musashi, Takuan and Yagyu in the sphere of the martial arts application of Zen theory, the central role of this point in practice is evident.

This realization is the pivot point of the Zen-budo path, the insight moment which leads to the phase transformation from flow to kensho.

To achieve this realization the veil of delusion will be pierced by some practitioners in the mind with senses withdrawn, by some through language, by others in action, but for all this is the threshold, the first glimpse of reality, the entry to the final stage of practice.

The Heart Sutra

Avalokiteshavara Bodhisattva, when deeply practicing prajna paramita, clearly saw that all five aggregates are empty and thus relieved all suffering.

Shariputra, form does not differ from emptiness; emptiness does not differ from form. Form itself is emptiness, emptiness itself form. Sensations, perceptions, formations, and consciousness are also like this.

Shariputra, all dharmas are marked by emptiness; they neither arise nor cease, are neither defiled nor pure, neither increase nor decrease. Therefore, given emptiness, there is **no** form, **no** sensation, **no** perception, **no** formation, **no** consciousness; **no** eyes, **no** ears, **no** nose, **no** tongue, **no** body, **no** mind; **no** sight, **no** sound, **no** smell, **no** taste, **no** touch, **no** object of mind; **no** realm of sight⋯ **no** realm of mind consciousness. There is neither ignorance nor extinction of ignorance⋯ neither old age and death, nor extinction of old age and death; **no** suffering, **no** cause, **no** cessation, **no** path; **no** knowledge and **no** attainment.

With nothing to attain, a bodhisattva relies on prajna paramita, and thus the mind is without hindrance. Without hindrance, there is no fear. Far beyond all inverted views, one realizes nirvana. All buddhas of past, present, and future rely on prajna paramita, and thereby attain unsurpassed, complete, perfect enlightenment.

Therefore, know the prajna paramita as the great miraculous mantra, the great bright mantra, the supreme mantra, the incomparable mantra, which removes all suffering and is true, not false.

Therefore, we proclaim the prajna paramita mantra, the mantra that says: "Gate Gate Paragate Parasamgate Bodhi Svaha."

Maka Hannya Haramita Shingyo

Kan ji zai bo satsu. Gyo jin han nya hara mita ji. Sho ken GO on kai ku. Do issai ku yaku. Sha ri shi. Shiki fu i ku. Ku fu i shiki. Shiki soku ze ku. Ku soku ze shiki. Ju so gyo shiki. Yaku bu nyo ze. Shari shi. Ze sho ho ku so. Fu sho fu metsu. Fu ku fu jo. Fu zo fu gen. Ze ko ku chu. **Mu** shiki **mu** ju so gyo shiki. **Mu** gen ni bi ze shin i. **Mu** shiki sho ko mi soku ho. **Mu** gen kai nai shi **mu** i shiki kai. **Mu mu** myo yaku **mu mu** myo jin. Nai shi mu ro shi. Yaku **mu** ro shi jin. **Mu** ku shu metsu do. **Mu** chi yaku **mu** toku. I **mu** sho toku ko. Bodai sat ta e hannya haramita KO Shin **mu** ke ge **mu** ke ge ko. **Mu**u ku fu. On ri issai ten do **mu** so. Ku gyo ne han. San ze sho butsu. E hannya haramita KO Toku a noku ta ra san myaku san bodai. Ko chi hannya haramita. Ze dai jin shu. Ze dai myo shu. Ze **mu** jo shu. Ze **mu** to do shu. No jo issai ku. Shin jitsu fu ko ko setsu hannya haramita shu. Soku setsu shu watsu. Gya tei, gya tei, HA ra gya tei. Hara so gya tei. BO ji so waka. Hannya Shingyo.

***

Note: To better understand the use of "no" in the Heart Sutra, and to understand the use of "mu" as a pointer to the emptiness of self-nature of persons and objects: A classic presentation of the distinction between material non-existence and sunyata, emptiness, is found in the Lam Rim Chen Mo by Tsongkhapa, in Volume III, Chapter 12. This treats the subject clearly, from a Mahayana perspective.

It is significant that the Heart Sutra is describing a gradual path of practice. It does not seem to be describing an "immediate enlightenment" doctrine. Soto Zen's immediate enlightenment case is presented in the meditation manual Fukanzazengi, compiled by Dogen, the 13th century founder of the Japanese Soto Zen school:

"To practice the Way singleheartedly is, in itself, enlightenment. There is no gap between practice and enlightenment ..."

The identity of practice and enlightenment form the core doctrine. There is nowhere to get to. There is no path to take. This seems to be understood to mean "just sit" and then "you" manifest perfect enlightenment.

In contrast, in the Heart Sutra, Avalokiteshvara, the personification of the cosmic principle of compassion, has been engaged in a gradual, developmental, mind training path to enlightenment. It seems he is engaged in meditation using the five aggregates or skandhas as his meditation object. The five skandhas – physical form, feelings, perceptions, volitions and consciousness – five of our fields of experience on which the views of self are constructed. Searching these five aggregates for a self is a formal meditation subject, set up in the early stratum of Buddhist practice, far earlier than the Heart Sutra. Avalokiteshvara "saw" emptiness. His insight is expressed in the past tense. He is in action: "doing deep prajna paramita" his mind searching for the nature of the five aggregates. There is a person, an object of attention, and an action. It sounds like there is a before and an after. There is practice and kensho.

The meditation he is doing is one of the Satipatthana Establishments of Mindfulness. He sees the no-self nature in the objects of his attention. He can see clearly because he has no hindrances in his mind. He removed the hindrances from his mind. Removing the hindrances – desire, ill-will, laxity, agitation, and doubt – according to early Buddhism, is the necessary gateway to deep concentration, which in turn gives a practitioner access to deep insight. The sutra includes these components which seem to form the practice sequence that Avalokiteshvara used to reach enlightenment.

The way some Zen practitioners resolve this presentation of a traditional, pre-Zen mode of practice, is through the doctrinal claim that they are manifesting this whole path now - in their posture and their practice of dropping off body and mind - although they seem to understand this in various ways. According to the way they express their understanding, to quote the Heart Sutra, there is no person, no path, and nothing to be attained. Without pretty good analytical tools it is hard to answer: Who is it that is doing the dropping off? What mind or body is there to drop off?

So, considering the dichotomy between the structure of the sutra and the doctrinal claims it makes, there is a tremendous opportunity for penetration of the truth by making the effort to resolve the apparent contradiction between the conventional view of the trainee and the reality of sunyata. There is, many people can tell you, no contradiction.

I never heard this subject matter taught or remarked upon. The Heart Sutra was used more as incantation than study guide.

The mantra at the end lists the stages of the path, from initiation to enlightenment. Beyond any analysis it has a dramatic, aural power too, beyond the words or ideas in it, from the sound of the chant. In 17 syllables the chant pulses, builds, repeats, comes to a climax, and tails off into silence. Stillness envelopes the room, as the sound fades to silence in the vast meditation hall. There is a lot there, in that emptiness.

Bodhidharma in China

Fifth century Indian Buddhist monk Bodhidharma, according to Zen legend, brought Zen to China. Chinese monk Hui K'e, was his disciple. Hui K'e pleaded with Bodhidharma to pacify his mind for him.

Bodhidharma said, **"Bring me your mind and I will pacify it for you."**

Hui K'e said, **"When I search for my mind, I cannot find it."**

Bodhidharma said, **"I have pacified your mind for you."** At this Hui K'e was enlightened.

That dialogue represents three stages of practice which unfolded between student and teacher over the course of years. It depicts the sudden result of long preparation. Because it is terse, naïve aspirants mistakenly think an exchange like this, with a perceptive teacher, can produce instant results. They also, mistakenly, believe the teacher produces the result.

The phase transition boundary to kensho, the path of seeing, is approached by an intense, persistent search for a "self." If no self can be found in or among any of the parts that make you up, if the searcher is absolutely certain that it is not there to be found, then your "no-self nature" is realized. This is outlined in the Heart Sutra.

This phase transition from flow or mushin begins at kensho and culminates at satori. In the Heart Sutra mantra's five step scheme Kensho is step three, and Satori is step five.

The flow state developed in martial practice is compared to samadhi in meditation. Samadhi is the concentration and tranquility that permits careful examination of the mind, without thoughts, ideas, perceptions or emotions interfering. Based on that tranquil concentration the tools of examination are used. These vary in different traditions, from the examination of the three marks of existence, the five skandhas or four elements, to analysis of phenomena based on their parts, the causes and conditions which bring them to being, the establishment of phenomena based on the language and mental habits of the observer, or the diamond drill, turning around again and again, shifting perspective in the mind, searching for the nature of the observer, and who it is who is being observed. These are a few. There are thousands of meditation subjects, practice paths, and manuals of instruction, which have been used for millennia throughout the world. But in all cases the search is mental, based on well-cultivated "samadhi," deep concentration, and uses techniques of "vipassana," insight, to access "prajna," liberative wisdom.

The problem with using the phrase "seeing your nature" to define this experience is that, in the understanding of this tradition, you don't have a fixed independent nature. You are to determine, conclusively, that it is not. That is the liberative insight, kensho.

This is not to say you don't exist. This is similar to the search for the center point of a turning wheel or for the present moment, which can be located relative to their context but in fact have no independent existence of their own. The liberative insight into the nature of the mind is similar.

Joshu's teacher said "Mu!" when asked about the dog's Buddha nature. He did not say that merely to "shock" Joshu. It was not intended to undercut the value of language. It was not to be mysterious, esoteric, inscrutable or heavy.

Joshu's teacher was giving the right answer to the question. Concise, but correct. As Joshu read and studied the prajna paramita sutras, the Heart Sutra and others, with their presentation of sunyata or emptiness, he would have encountered the negation of self-nature endlessly repeated, from many perspectives. The Heart Sutra uses "Mu" again and again to make the point that things have "no-self." Mu IS the dog's Buddha nature. The fact that no thing has a fixed nature, but rather all are processes, always changing. Things are perceived, labeled, but are limitless in their range of engagement with their causes, conditions, and parts and with the perceptions and karma of each of their observers. That is the nature a Buddha has. That is what Buddha nature is. That does not mean a dog is a Buddha. It does not mean that a dog is not a dog. It does not deny that a dog will really bark, bite or be happy to see you.

It means a dog exists with the same fundamental metaphysical relationship to the cosmos that a Buddha does: no intrinsic unchanging independent self. In light of this, over infinite lives, over infinite eons, the karmic continuum of this dog will always have a Buddha nature, and it will at some future moment of the continuum of his mindstream, see his own Buddha nature.

Or he may be a Buddha now, who you see as a dog. (See the story of Arya Asanga and his rescue of the sick and dying dog, who he discovers is the future Buddha, Maitreya who he was dying to see.)

Buddha nature means we do not have a fixed nature. We are always changing. We act, we are subject to conditions, we change. There is no intrinsic self-existence in things or people. Understanding that is mu. Seeing that yourself is kensho.

Where to look? The Heart Sutra lists the parts of a person – the list of things negated in the Heart Sutra includes several lists of these components. A doctrinally trained, practiced meditator can recite the Heart Sutra and use the lists to consider each component of their body and mind in turn and could search for a "self" in each of them and not find it, or you might say, recognize the no-self in them.

In the Zen tradition the word "mind" is used for the object of this search. In Zen, as distinct from other traditions which use reason to access wisdom, the mind is not engaged in rational analysis and search. They use other techniques. But the phase transition threshold – to the path of seeing, kensho – is said to be the same.

The word the translator uses in the Hui K'e exchange above, to describe passing the phase transition boundary, is "enlightened." This word is used with a range of definitions in Zen – often without distinguishing the third phase, kensho, from the culminating fifth phase, satori, also called nirvana or Buddhahood. This is a source (and sometimes a result) of confusion.

If the words in this dialogue – **"Pacify my mind for me…"** etc. – were exchanged between unprepared people, they would be meaningless. For Hui K'e, searching desperately for his mind as instructed, finding nothing on which to pin the word "mind", having exhausted every possibility, having looked everywhere, having reached the end of his rope, these words from his teacher meant everything.

Having searched for his mind while believing it was a fixed thing, with a fixed set of characteristics, i.e., with a nature of its own, his mind became turbulent. Suddenly seeing it as empty – i.e., without a permanent, rigid form, without rigid boundaries, without a rigid nature, without an inner pilot-homunculus, without a little owner-operator in there anywhere, finding it empty of self-nature – in a breathtaking, transformative moment of deliverance, the intense pressure of concentration is suddenly released, long mental habits drop away, the scale of his perspective goes from personal to universal, and he suddenly finds vivid, all-encompassing peace.

The process in this story matches the others used in Zen and in Zen-budo. Can martial arts do this?

Yagyu Munenori's Three Phase System

The pivotal moment in this story of the Diamond Sutra master's exchange with his teacher, the tea lady, is presented as a kensho, a first direct seeing of the nature of mind which begins the final stage of the path to complete liberation. With this understanding we can take a look at the claims of Zen-budo as a path leading to liberation.

Earlier we took a look at Takuan Soho's Zen instruction to sword master Yagyu Munenori. Yagyu Munenori was the teacher of the Tokugawa shogun Iyemitsu, the military dictator of Japan.

Yagyu took Takuan's advice and created his own interpretation of it. Yagyu's theory of the path to the mastery of swordsmanship, written as a private document for his family and students, is divided into three parts, which map onto the typologies of phase transformation I have presented.

His section titles outline his conception of the three stages of transformation:

> 1. "The Killing Sword," which deals with the use of force;

2. "The Life-Giving Sword," which focuses on preventing conflict.

3. "No Sword," Yagyu's final chapter, reflects the approach of his Zen teacher Takuan Soho and his near-contemporary Musashi Miyamoto. The name No Sword is a reference to Mu, a pointer to the central insight in Zen theory.

The "No Sword" chapter presents the ultimate achievement of the sword master: action without volition, beyond any calculation or perceptions which will halt the mind and impede the action of the swordsman. At this third stage the swordsman is not separate from the gestalt in any way – body, mind, action, attack, defense, opponent and the sword itself are all functioning as a single undivided event. He is an active manifestation of no-self nature, in Yagyu's view.

This echoes the view of the Mind Only tenet school of Buddhism, which is associated with Bodhidharma's introduction of the Lankavatara Sutra to China. This school emphasizes the unity of subject, object and action – warrior, opponent and technique, in this example – arising from a single karma, existing as a unity, each component entailing the others.

The three stages in Yagyu's letter are presented by Yagyu as ascending stages. These stages are considered within the tradition to indicate the path to total mastery.

As expressed, they map the path to the high flow state of mastery and possibly beyond. This is an extraordinarily high achievement. It is very rare. Can they lead to liberation? The achievement, as he expresses it, seems to remain within the boundaries of this world. Can we avoid the conclusion that, good or bad, the warrior will carry his karma – the consequences of his volitional action – with him beyond death? Yagyu is addressing warlords and mercenaries, not saints or monks.

Appendix Two

The issue of Kata and Seizing

Our approach to interpretation restores the effectiveness of karate technique, including basic kihon, which have been practiced in the dojo but have not been used, or useful, in kumite or combatives.

There are seven "down block" or gedan uke combinations in our first kata, Fukyugata ichi, the kata Sensei Nagamine created. With the possible exception of the first move, none can be understood as blocking a low attack. That is because they involve a turn to the rear.

Note: There will be video demos on our website for all the techniques and bunkai interpretations described in this book.

A good way to make these moves actually work with correct timing and distance is to use them to counter a grab by trapping and throwing, and then following up with a punch, as the kata shows.

This same move can also be used against a punch from in front of you, by repositioning the body out of the line of attack, rerouting the incoming punch or kick, and as against the grab, trapping the attacking arm or leg, and using the pivot to throw the opponent.

The second to third move, for example: You punch. If it is effective you win. If your arm is grabbed when punching, and your opponent begins to execute and lock or throw, it might be possible to roll out or to go the ground. Or you could do what we do: drop your center, trap the opponent's grabbing arm against you, pull him in and throw him over your hip as you turn.

If there is too much resistance to do it, that is if you were too slow to disrupt his balance, then you could follow up instantly with strikes. But we learn to make this work.

The follow up finishing technique after the 180° turn and throw, in this example, is a middle punch, targeting at solar plexus height. (What the actual target is on the body of the opponent is not specified, as his position at this point will not be predictable.)

In Pinan Nidan, similar to Heian Shodan in Shotokan and other styles, this sequence appears again, identically, but it is followed up differently. Here is it followed by an attempt to grab and lock your punch. With your right-hand punch grabbed you could go to the ground, you could try to roll out, or you could try to leap over your opponent to release the pressure applied to your grabbed arm.

You could also do what we train to do: drop fast into nekko ashi dachi, jolt the attacker off balance toward you, break the attacker's wrist grab with a strike to his stretched wrist tendons.

Then, as he is falling toward you, immediately reverse direction and counter attack with a punch. Which is what is in the kata.

High speed reversal and full-body coordination are required to pull this off. That is why we train in the use of the waist to reverse direction, from day one. And as a result, we do not need to roll out, leap, or go to the ground.

Defense Against Grabs and Throws

Throwing techniques start in first kata. Anti-throwing techniques start in first kata too. One example, of many, comes one count before the kiai move, as we turn from the fifth direction to the sixth, from a "high block" to the reverse punch, kiai move.

After the opponent tries to punch your face, you block him by rerouting his incoming punch past your face, using your crossing arm. He continues his attack, continuing his forward motion, and immediately dropping the elbow of his blocked, raised arm to your chest for an elbow strike. As he does this he steps, placing his left foot behind yours, to trip or sweep you, attempting to push you over his left leg.

The kata teaches a counter to this technique: we side step, contact his knee with our knee, then we quickly rotate our waist to make the 45° turn, forcing his knee to bend against the natural range of the joint, displacing his foot, and spinning his body backward, leaving his back now facing us. Then we strike.

This works quickly and efficiently, without changing the kata, and with a genuine flow of combative intention and exchange of energy from each opponent. This move teaches a useful defensive option, and is interesting to work on, instead of just accepting this sequence as a piece of choreography.

It is also good preparation for the effective and more difficult anti-throw in Pinan shodan. That one is similar. It begins at the fourth chudan shuto, stepping into the kosa dachi chudan uke technique.

Pinan Shodan Builds on This

There are notable throws in Pinan shodan. The three-quarter turn after the nukite kiai move, for example, has no practical combative meaning if it is asking you to turn 270° backwards to your left in order to discover a new opponent who was standing 90° to your right.

However, if you use the preceding sequence of "knife hand chest blocks" to 1. stop a punch and then 2. trap, 3. elbow lock, and 4. break your opponent's balance, bending him forward as he attempts to grab your right wrist – then your nukite kiai move makes sense.

You instantly step in, closing the grabbed hand and snapping it back into the chamber releasing his grip, and drawing his left side toward you with his arm extended and his arm pit kyusho unprotected. At the same time, you snap your right hand open forming a nukite. This spear hand thrust is then set up to naturally penetrate his exposed arm pit. In training we do not do this target penetration. It might sound like this would be complex artificial choreography but it takes no planning. The technique sequence works naturally and makes sense.

To follow up you just close your hand to seize his pectoral muscle for a muscle separation chin na technique, (or for training purposes you grab his gi), pull him down to your side with your right arm and control his head with your left, as you step back and throw, using the three-quarter turn.

The move works, it makes sense, and you can use any of the parts of the technique sequence as individual techniques, or in other combinations.

Pinan Kata Start by Countering Grappling

The initial moves of the five Pinan kata make sense as defenses against standard attacks used in grappling arts. Our quick response is designed to disrupt and counter them – ideally before the grab is fully locked on, but they can work even if the grab is completed.

Two of these – the first moves of Pinan Sandan and Godan - can be applied to a punch from the front. But defending against a single front punch to the middle of the body without a control technique or a decisive counter is not a good tactical choice. It is useful to explore beyond that.

For the first move of Pinan Shodan your left wrist and right shoulder are seized by your opponent, who attempts to step in behind our left leg for a reaping sweep or throw. We do the first move of Pinan Shodan, closing the distance, bending his arms and then, with the drop and pivot, breaking the opponent's grip, balance and body architecture.

Then we use our high arm to strike down on the proximate target – one of his arms, the back of his neck (if he bent forward, or the thumb tendons of his exposed wrist if he attempts to seize your wrist) – destabilizing his balance, snapping his head back, and following with the right-hand punch shown in the kata, as the decisive finishing technique.

This interpretation is one of many valid ones. It is effective and it precisely matches the kata.

The sequences of two, three or four knife-hand shuto techniques have no real application against two or three or four punches in a row. The attacker would have to be walking backward, while maintaining a steady and ineffective distance from you.

That is silly. These sequences work very well as a series in which a technique appears to be repeated but is a varied use of a single pattern of movements.

These sequences occur in Pinan Shodan and kata Wankan and elsewhere, can begin with a rising knife-hand used to intercept a punch or a grab toward the middle of your body, a re-routing block sending the incoming limb past you, where you can apply a joint lock, and then follow with a throw, joint dislocation or take down.

This karate is multi-dimensional. It is a revival of the pre-20th century karate that was designed on Okinawa.

This may seem brutal. To defend against pirates in the China Sea up close and personal was brutal. That was not similar to dojo karate or school fitness karate or even Japanese college karate clubs. As vigorous and intense and transformative and great as all that can be, the mindset that gave rise to te in the olden days, defending life and livelihood on ships and in foreign ports, was like the violence of gangs, cartels and warlords. We may not want to think like them or live like them. But the techniques are in the kata. We are not learning only to parry and strike.

We Counter the Intention of the Attacker – Not Just Techniques

Our grappling counters work naturally in dynamic situations – where the attacker is moving aggressively, seizing, attempting to destabilize us, and positioning for a throw. In the unlikely event that an assailant grabs your wrist and shoulder and stands there looking at you – not likely – a well-focused fist, a foot or knee to a vital target might resolve the threat.

But in the continuum of motion, you will need to reposition to disrupt the flow of his intended attack. The first moves of all the Pinan kata use a flanking movement to the opponent's left side to accomplish this.

First Move Release

For Pinan Nidan (Shotokan's Heian Shodan) our interpretation assumes that you would not be standing still in a formal yoi position, arms extended straight down, while an aggressor is putting his hands on you. You probably wouldn't.

However, we do include the yoi position in our interpretation of the move. If you were in a high guard position, with your arms up, ready to strike and defend, your hands closed in front of your chest and face, it may happen that an opponent will grab your front wrist, or knock it down, attempting to jab over it.

He might grab your front wrist and attempt to throw you by hanging on to your front wrist, pulling you toward him, stepping back, sinking, locking your arm against his body, hyperextending your elbow, and rotating out.

Yoi as a Part of a Continuum for Interpretation

To prevent that from happening, from the high guard fighting posture, when the opponent grabs your front wrist, we can drop the left fist sharply straight down, moving through the yoi position of the left arm. That breaks the hold or snaps the opponent forward if he is hanging on.

By circling that arm back up to your right shoulder, as the kata has it, you bring your wrist on top of his for a wrist release. If it releases you counter. If he hangs on this move bends him further forward, his head bent close to you, and takes him off his balance for a split second.

Before he recovers his balance, your hammer fist stuns to the temple or other available target. The next move, the step in and punch, is the finishing technique.

Long Throw

In Pinan Nidan we use the series of three "high blocks" as a stop, trap and throw sequence. It works, without changing the kata at all. The alternative – that the opponent is walking backwards while trying to punch you in the face three times and then, after the third attempt fails, runs away, is a suboptimal interpretation of this kata sequence.

No one with experience outside the dojo would assume you could pull an assaultive opponent's punch out of the air and manipulate it while they are fully energized and attacking. But if they attempt to grab us, as they trained to do, or attempt to clinch as they are tiring out, that may be possible.

"Repeated" "Defensive" Techniques

The most straightforward and practical interpretations of Pinan Sandan do not include defenses against a punch anywhere in the kata, and against kicks just twice. We use punches and other strikes to counterattack, as finishing techniques. Pinan Sandan teaches effective anti-grappling techniques, throwing counters, and lock-releasing techniques, from beginning to end. The influence of Okinawan sumo, (also known as tegumi 手組, SUMAI 角力, and shima シマ) is evident.

The first move of Pinan Sandan works naturally against contact to the chest: a grab of the gi at the lapel to set up a throw or to pull you into a punch, or an attempt to shove you back by pushing your chest. (The first move of Pinan Sandan can work against a punch from the front too, but not as well, even if your technique turns him, because it leaves the opponent standing in front of you and free to move when you are dropped into a low stance, while your next move in the kata does not apply readily to anything you would want to do with an intact, aggressive opponent instantly following up.)

In Pinan Sandan, when the opponent grabs your lapel at the center of the chest, or shoves your chest back with his palm, we step towards him as we pin his contact arm against our chest, immobilizing it as you step toward him. That's the first half of the "chest block" at the beginning of the kata. His head falls forward as you move.

The second half of the "chest block" happens as you drop and pivot. It is not a chest block. It functions as a backfist to the temple, (or to the side of the neck as a brachial stun, or to the mandibular angle, whichever head-target comes into the line of the attack.) Another high backfist and groin strike follow up. This works well and matches the moves of the kata.

That's a sample of the way we investigate these moves and how we train with them: prevent or trap the grab or reroute the incoming punch, destabilizing the opponent and following up with a decisive counter.

Receiving Power

The kata teach this sequence when an opponent's power is projected toward us. That is when we are receiving incoming energy from the attacker. Uke, 受, means receiving.

Projecting Power

When we are projecting power there is another tactic taught by the kata: to instantly fill the void, or cover the gap in our defense, created by our power projection.

Our Fukyugata Ni, created by Miyagi Chojun, also a part of the Goju Ryu curriculum, trains us to be alert for the weak points created in any move or posture that we use, and teaches us how to defend against an able opponent's exploitation of that suki, or gap in our defense. Simple example: when our hands are high, as they are after the first and fourth move, the attack comes in low. We train to defend that suki, by immediately dropping into a low defense to counter.

When we are fully extended, as in the zenkutsu dachi gedan zuki, a long, low stance with our punch fully committed to the front, we are generating maximum power and body stability, but only toward the front –

we are vulnerable from the rear. For example, a bear hug applied by a new opponent coming up behind us, pinning our arms to our sides, in an attempt to take us down. Another vulnerability of this posture is our Achilles tendon, exposed and stretched behind us.

Through good kata bunkai analysis we learn to defend against both of those possibilities. We do it by using the next move in the kata, and we learn to exploit the new opportunity which we set up. In this kata we are repeatedly taught to be alert to potential vulnerabilities, seen or unseen, especially from directly behind us.

Toward the end of the kata, when we are extended high in a shizentai dachi with a knife hand extended to the side, our opponent may drop under our strike and instantly lunge in for a tackle.

Our posture is susceptible to that attack. As in rock-paper-scissors, in kumite, everything is susceptible to something. Miyagi Chojun was teaching how to counter tackling, used in Okinawan sumo and modern grappling systems.

His solution, as shown in the next move of the kata, is to pivot back out of range into a new zenkutsu dachi, forward leaning stance, low and long for stability front to back. As we move into this new position, we reroute the attacker's reaching arms with what looks like a "chest block": our arms cross our center line at the mid-level of the body, and instantly follow up with a strike to his jaw or head. That's all a precise interpretation of the movement in this kata. Nothing needs to be modified at all. This kata's instruction in practical combative skill is very valuable. It is not hidden.

Splitting

The splitting moves and knee lifts, especially when used together – as in Rohai, Passai and the Naihanchi katas are effective against a grappling attack.

The hand technique plus simultaneous knee lifts in Wankan, Wanshu and Gojushiho makes sense when interpreted this way too. A knee lift can block a kick, but used simultaneously with the hand techniques in these kata, that interpretation does not work quite as well.

Our Objective is not Submission or Arrest

We do not apply restraint holds, submission techniques or pain compliance techniques to complete a defense in our kata.

We do not take an opponent to the ground to pin or immobilize them. Our kata are designed to train us for defensive combatives, not competition, arrest, or military commando assault.

Our Objective is to Stop the Threat

Karate is sometimes interpreted in ways which are inconsistent with what is taught in the kata. In karate kumite for example, karateka sometimes face off like boxers.

But the kata do not teach boxing, or kick boxing. Inspired by what they have seen or learned, some karateka try to clinch and go to the ground.

Shoshin Nagamine founder of Matsubayashi Ryu, the predecessor style of Yamabayshi Ryu, was a long-time public official and one time Chief of Police.

He was a San dan, third-degree black belt, in judo. Judo, by his time, had replaced jiu jitsu as the taiho-jitsu – the subject control and arrest technique system – taught throughout Japan to police cadets and officers.

As shown on my Go dan, fifth-degree black belt diploma – he called his training center a "Kodokan" – the term for lecture hall – which was also the name used for the Japanese national training center for judo.

Sensei Nagamine was a lifetime karate practitioner. He was also well-versed in judo's methods of going to the ground, and using the ground when you got there. He advised his karate students not to go to the ground.

He emphasized maintaining balance, and staying on your feet. Sensei Funakoshi, also a Shorin Ryu practitioner, included the throwing techniques found in the kata as an important part of his curriculum. He did not teach going to the ground.

In law enforcement, when subject restraint and arrest are the goals, the ground may be a necessary piece of the tactical puzzle. Under other circumstances, it is not an advantageous place to be. The ground is not mats. It is rocks, gravel, pavement, steps, curbs, broken glass, needles, garbage, many surprises.

On the ground, however skilled you may be, you have reduced use of personal weapons and you lose defensive options that are accessible when you are on your feet. You are also vulnerable to your attacker's friends, any or all of whom may choose to kick a field goal with your head. Ground fighting is a good skill. It has its place on the tactical spectrum.

We train to stay on our feet. Our kata show this.

As we apply the kata bunkai, use kumite and other modes of training, and drawing on our own experience, we can tell that this was not an omission but a combative approach, a mindset and tactical toolkit, designed to keep us alive.

Means of Attack

People get attacked. Victims of robbery, rape, assault live with the memory for a long time. People fight over insults, rude looks, respect, drugs, debts, money, girlfriends, a team. Sometimes two guys go face to face and have at it. But most attacks come out of nowhere. A punch to the back of the head, a confrontation and threat, a weapon in the hand of a stranger. Sometimes people grab, hold on and try to take the other guy down – using the tactics of current martial culture. People see it in matches and entertainment. Grappling arts were predominant long ago, when our kata were devised.

Military Doctrine Reflects and Reinforces Popular Trends in Personal Defense

Military hand to hand doctrine has tracked with the evolution of popular martial arts. This trend is relevant to what we – professional or civilian – encounter. At one time boxing was the predominant fighting art. When the Marine Corps Martial Arts Program was coming together, Marines, stationed on Okinawa, learned from top practitioners there, and Okinawan karate had a growing reputation stateside as the real thing.

Currently the Army prioritizes grappling for new soldiers. Army manual STP 21-1-SMCT, Warrior Skills, Level 1, outlines the approach:

071-000-0006 React to Man-to-Man Contact

1. Achieve the clinch.
Note: Controlling a standup fight means controlling the range between fighters. The untrained fighter is primarily dangerous at punching range. The goal is to avoid that range. Even if you are the superior striker, the most dangerous thing you can do is to spend time at the range where the opponent has the highest probability of victory.

a. Close the gap and achieve the clinch.

(1) Start from a fighting stance outside of the kicking range.

(2) Tuck in your chin and use the arms to cover the vital points of your head.

(3) Aggressively close the distance.

(4) Place your head to the opponent's chest and your cupped hands to the opponent's biceps.

(5) Aggressively fight for one of the following dominant clinch positions ⋯then attempt a takedown to the ground ⋯then achieve dominant body position, guard, mount or side ⋯then finish using chokes, arm bar⋯

We Defend Against This Approach

This matches the tactics of wrestling arts like Okinawan sumo and contemporary grappling arts. It fits the trajectory of a combative encounter as fighters use up their initial burst of ATP energy and begin to grab and restrain the opponent. Our traditional kata give us the techniques and tactics we use to defend against this.

Beyond skill, to prevail against grappling attacks, or any attack, requires endurance, will and aggression, which are cultivated in training.

To defend – against a boxer, a sport fighter, someone enraged or intoxicated, desperate or insane, whether they are on their feet swinging, closing the distance for a tackle, grab or throw, attempting to get their arms to

your neck or their hands to your throat – is what we train to do. Properly decoded, and properly trained, our kata give us tools to deal with deadly combative problems.

***

One Unique Technique

Naihanchi body mechanics are in some important ways distinct from the body mechanics of our other kata.

There are two foot and leg techniques in naihanchi kata. They have distinct functions.

When stepping side to side we snap our knee up. It is a knee strike when the opponent is in close contact range.

At a slightly longer range it might be used as a blocking technique. It can also be used to avoid a sweep. These applications exist in many kata.

The one unique technique that appears only in naihanchi is the foot sweep, used when we are stationary. It can be used as a single strike, the upward sweep of your foot used to target the attacker's knee joint, nerve points, and other leg targets. It can be used as a double strike, by following up the rising strike with an attack to the opponent's shin, ankle or foot, on the downward phase of the sweep, as it returns to the ground.

This foot sweep is used to destabilize the opponent, break his balance and disorient him, creating a momentary opportunity for a decisive follow up technique. This is built in to the design of the kata. It is a key component of the tactics that naihanchi teaches.

These two naihanchi foot techniques – the knee lift while traveling and the foot sweep while in place – have two distinct modes of execution as well.

The first is clear cut and familiar. The mode of execution of the knee strike when traveling in naihanchi is similar to any kicking or knee strike technique in any other kata: snap the waist forward on the same side as the knee you are launching, and lift the foot without weight transfer or pause. Nothing unusual. It is quick and strong.

Some people launch the second naihanchi leg technique, the foot sweep in place, in the same way – by releasing the naihanchi isometric tension, and throwing the foot. But there is another way to do it which is unique. It is faster and stronger. We have no other technique that works the same way.

Because it is unique its properties are easy to miss. This reduces the effectiveness of the technique, and of naihanchi training in general.

Here is how to get the most out of it: The energy generation principle in the foot sweep technique is similar to firing a catapult, or triggering the jaws of a trap. It is a release of pre-loaded, potential energy.

The mechanism – in our case the leg – is held under full tension before the technique is launched. This is unlike all our other techniques – blocks, punches, kicks, throws, seizing, etc. – where we generate a pulse of power to initiate the technique. The naihanchi foot sweep technique, already under its full load of potential energy, is ready to fire.

This depends on doing the naihanchi posture with the whole body from head to toe, unified under isometric tension, with proper alignment, as described above. It especially relies on the unique naihanchi architecture of the legs.

If the feet are placed on top of the floor or ground, passively, the technique will not work as designed.

In fact, the naihanchi stance itself will not serve its function. Even if the legs are tight and the feet are drawn toward each other over the surface of the floor or ground – it still won't work well.

What is necessary is to form a fully "arched" integrated body structure, which will include as its base a fully arched, unified leg structure. Without moving them, the legs are pulled toward each other, using the inner leg muscles to create a pincer. The feet are pulled into the ground and rotated so that the pressure on the heels will push the heels toward each other, and the pressure on the front of the foot would rotate the toes outward, away from each other, if they were free to move. The legs create a circle of energy that feels like it is reaching under the ground.

A good naihanchi stance should feel like you are seizing the earth with your feet, using the leg arch.

The isometric tension created by the foot rotation and the gluteus and adductor tension makes a strong, coherent structure.

Its stability is enhanced by using the pelvis as the keystone of the arch, connecting the legs;

by keeping the pelvis in a neutral position front to back; and by forming a barrel shape with the lower abdominal muscles, centered at the dan tien, rather than pulling the abdomen in, or swelling it out, to harden it.

These are some of the key components of an optimal naihanchi lower body structure.

This structure is testable in a number of ways. It can be checked with strikes or pressure to the legs in all directions, and with other applications of shimēi – body striking and pressure – waza, and bunkai.

The definitive test of a sound naihanchi stance is to check if the body is well-rooted front to back. That is: see if, when under pressure to the front of the body, you can maintain the naihanchi posture without either tipping back, buckling at the center, or leaning forward into the pressure. If you are doing it well your stance will remain stable and firm under direct or angled pressure from the front.

Naihanchi stance is easy to make stable side to side.

That can be done with muscle strength. To make naihanchi – a wide, shallow stance – stable from front to back, takes good technique.

The tactical utility of stability under pressure from the front is this: if we are struck or grabbed from the front, or if we seize or strike an opponent in front of us, especially when there is no room or time to retreat or rotate out, we can remain stable long enough to take the power and respond, as we move laterally to the follow up position, to seize or strike. Under bunkai analysis it is clear that is how the naihanchi kata combative tactics are designed. No modifications of the kata pattern are necessary to get these interpretations to work.

Without this front to back stability under dynamic pressure you have to interpret naihanchi tactics to involve body shifting and repositioning – similar to all the other katas we do. There is none of that in naihanchi embusen.

If you interpret naihanchi as teaching a way of responding when you cannot retreat,

for example if your back is to a wall, the principle is critical. Getting pinned to a wall, off balance, when your opponent is alert, energized and attacking, is not good.

Front to back stability while maintaining side to side stability – what we do in naihanchi – gives us the rootedness to respond to these combative dynamics, and enables us to move side to side, without a loss of balance or root, so we do not get pinned or destabilized under pressure.

Because of the dynamic tension built into the architecture of the body in naihanchi, the unique foot-sweep in-place technique gives us a valuable defensive weapon. We will not make the most of this body weapon if we take the time to shift our balance and body weight over to the opposite leg, in order to snap our striking foot and leg up. It is unique in our kata.

This is a sample of our interpretations, an overview of our approach to kata bunkai investigation, and its application to practical training.

***

You should know, at every moment, that your life is essential. The world needs you. I hope that in your karate you will discover a spring that is always flowing fresh and clear, no matter how much you draw from it, no matter how many people come to share with you what you have found.

Jeffrey Brooks
Spring, 2023

True Karate Dō

Now, people feel surrounded. Good people feel disoriented, alone, uncertain of what to do. Like an elk in the woods scenting wolves. Like a ship in the sea as the waves climb higher. Like a baker in Constantinople long ago whose bread for years scented the sweet morning air who now breathes the smoke of the city on fire. Like a carpenter in Rome who made good houses, good furniture, good tools for people, wondering what use there will be for his wood and his nails.

People now witness the tide of ignorance drowning reason, kindness and life. They feel the frenzy blaze across the land, a fire whose time has come.

What do we do? We do not throw away our lives, or cling to them. We use them for what they are for. We use the great kata and conform our lives to it. We train ourselves to meet its ideals:

Generosity – Give people what you can and what they need.

Morality – Control your impulses, and show people consideration and respect.

Patience – Persist in doing what's right, one step at a time, without anger.

Effort – Persist in doing what's right and never, ever give up.

Concentration – Train your mind to be stable and calm and clear.

Wisdom – Train your mind to penetrate the truth, completely.

This does not mean be nice. It means be determined and courageous in virtue. We persist until we can say "I have done what had to be done."

There is something else in the rising wind. It is spring. It is beyond life and death. It is ours.

You cannot just do it. Train it and practice it.

Then just do it.

Train well.

Glossary

Here are some definitions of terms that may be unfamiliar. Most are defined the first time they appear in the book. One thing about these words is that it is not always clear what different people are using them to mean.

If we are using a noun, especially if it points to something we care about, it is pretty easy to grasp the meaning, and use the word effectively. If you are living in the countryside or the woods and you are hungry and someone says there are some blueberries over there, you will understand. It will matter.

There are different kinds of blueberries. There are ripe ones and tart ones and old ones and perfect ones, and you can't tell from the speaker which they are. But you get the general idea of what is there and you can go there and eat some. The words will point closely to something that you can understand.

Later if someone says there is a wolf over there, that matters, you do not want to be eaten, the communication is clear enough to act upon, you understand and use the words and ideas, and go the other way. What type of wolf, how many, young or old, hungry or full – those questions are not answered, but they can wait.

But with states of mind, it is harder to be clear. And with labels for states of mind translated from other languages it is more obscure. Especially if the technical vocabulary is not standardized and the same foreign word is rendered in multiple ways in English, and the nuances vary.

It is even more confusing if the states referred to are not mental states you have experienced, but which interest you, which you would like to explore, but which you need to imagine based on experiences you have had, and attempt to infer from them what the new mental state would be like. That makes language hard to use well.

Some of the most familiar terms in spiritual practice are like this. There is no one standard definition for many of these terms, and they are used by different writers, practitioners, teachers, translators and traditions in different ways.

I will take a crack at making my use of them clear, and when I am quoting from sources in various traditions, I have made an effort to point out the divergences in usage, and the significance of these differences.

One set of terms that is confusing is liberation, enlightenment, realization, awakening, insight, Buddhahood and nirvana.

There are technical sets that describe steps on the path to deeper spiritual maturity in the early Buddhist understanding: worldling, trainee, stream enterer, once returner, non-returner, arhat.
These have specific technical definitions which describe the negative mental states, the hindrances, fetters, and asavas, which cease at each successive level.

In the Zen traditions sometimes kensho and satori are used to differentiate between the first glimpse of the nature of reality, or of emptiness, called kensho, and the complete enduring realization, complete enlightenment, called satori. These do not have such specific descriptions and are described allusively, if at all.

What is most important for this book is that based on these technical differences it is clear that the use of the terms "awakening", "enlightenment" and "liberation" in the east Asian martial arts traditions, assessed on the basis of the statements and actions of the practitioners, is not the same as the early Buddhist or many later traditions' use of these terms.

For our purposes, what we can do is investigate what to do and what to avoid. We can determine what constitutes wholesome action with good results, and what constitutes unwholesome action with harmful results.

With this in mind we can get the guidance we need to pursue our goals, and use language as a tool, where there is shared interest and understanding, to refine our experience and action.

Abhisamayalamkara – a Mahayana Sanskrit prajna paramita treatise, central in Tibet

Asavas – the craving for sense pleasures, craving for existence and ignorance

Avalokiteshvara   Cosmic Bodhisattva of Compassion

Avatamsaka – The main text in Sanskrit of the Hua Yen school; Kegon Kyo in Japanese

Bhikkhu – An ordained Buddhist monastic, in Pali

Ba Gua – A Chinese Taoist eight component symbol set representing cosmic polarities

Bodhisattva – A person or transcendent being on the path to Buddhahood

Budo - 武道 -   Japanese for Martial Arts, literally "War Way"

Buddha – the Awakened One, Siddhartha Gautama, in India, 5th C. BCE, one of a series

Bun Bu Ryo Dō – The way of both civil life and war

Bunkai – Analysis of the fighting applications of kata by dividing and examining moves

Ch'an – Chinese meditation schools originating in the 6th C. Zen in Japanese

Damatte keiko – Shut up and train

Dharma – The teaching of the Buddha; the way things exist; phenomena

Dhyana – Sanskrit for meditation. Also, single pointed absorption.

Dō – Path, Way, Tao

Dojo – Place where the way is practiced

Emptiness – Sanskrit sunyata, the essential liberative insight in Mahayana

Enlightenment – Awakening to the true nature of reality, the cessation of ignorance and disturbance

Enso – Zen circle used to symbolize emptiness

Flow state – Activity that is energized, focused, effortless, skillful, challenging, concentrated, and elevated.

Gandavyuha – a chapter of the Kegon Kyo (Japanese), Avatamsaka (Sanskrit) or Flower Ornament Sutra, an Indian Mahayana sutra, depicting the path to enlightenment.

Hara – the physical center of the body in the lower abdomen; a reservoir of energy.

Hua Yen School – Chinese Mahayana school based in the Avatamsaka sutra.

Insight – Multiple definitions include intellectual understanding reality, direct perception of reality, the practice of vipassana or insight meditation to analyze the nature of reality.

Jhana – Pali pronunciation of Dhyana (Sanskrit), meditation, or a deep, single-pointed meditative absorption

Jitsu – Japanese, meaning art or skill or technique

Kansha – Japanese, Gratitude

Karate – Japanese, Empty hand, which originated on Okinawa

Karate-ka – Japanese, Karate practitioner

Kata – Japanese, Form, a karate term for a technique training sequence

Kihon – Japanese, Basic components

Kegon – Japanese, the Hua Yen school

Kensho – The first glimpse of the nature of reality. Also called the path of seeing in Mahayana, and Stream Entry in Theravada. This is the threshold moment of liberative insight which will proceed to nirvana or complete enlightenment. The insight is described as direct perception of the four noble truths, or of emptiness, or the cessation (in this case temporarily) of the asavas.

Koan – Japanese, a "public case" or puzzling question put to a Zen student for reflection and penetration.

Koshi – Japanese, waist. The mechanical center of the body.

Kumite – Japanese, "crossing hands" used a term for sparring and two-person training drills.

Kyusho – Japanese, the weak points in the body which are especially vulnerable to attack.

Lam Rim Chen Mo – The Great Stages of the Path to Enlightenment, an influential Tibetan Gelug school treatise, 15th C., by Tsongkapa

Liberation – This is used in multiple ways. It can refer to kensho, the first glimpse of reality which inevitably leads to complete awakening, it can refer to satori, the completion of the path of awakening. The structure of the path to enlightenment in different traditions varies, and the definitions of the stages does as well. It is sometimes used to describe reality here and now. It is understood in the tradition that what binds us to suffering, what imprisons us in the endless wandering in samsaric existence, is craving, based on ignorance and the resulting pursuit of misunderstood objects of desire. So liberation can be understood as freedom from ignorance, freedom from craving, freedom from the terrible consequences of unskillful actions taken in pursuit of misunderstood objects of desire.

Madhyamaka – the Middle Way school, founded by 2nd C. Indian monk Nagarjuna

Mahayana – the Great Vehicle, the school uses the Bodhisattva path ideal, the messianic drive to save all beings as the motive for the accumulation of the wisdom and skill to do it.

Majjhima Nikaya – An early collection of the sermons of the Buddha and chief disciples.

Mantra – A set of words or sounds believed by some to have special spiritual power.

Matsubayashi Ryu – the Pine Forest Style of Okinawan Shorin Ryu karate, assembled by Nagamine Shoshin in the mid 20th C. It is the predecessor style of Yamabayashi Ryu

Menkyo Kaiden – Menkyo is a teaching license used in some Japanese traditional arts. Kaiden refers to the transmission of the entire system.

Mindfulness – Sati in Sanskrit. Intentionally bringing the attention to some aspect of the present time – to the body, the feelings, the mind, or phenomena. It is used to develop concentration and applied to insight practices.

Mu – Japanese particle of negation.

Mushin – No mind, sometimes empty mind, sometimes used to describe a state where cognition, intention, past and present subside allowing action to be spontaneous.

Naihanchi – A set of three kata which use isometric tension and special body postures to unify the body structure and condition deep solidity throughout the body.

Nikaya – Sanskrit. Collections of early Buddhist teachings.

Nin Tai – Japanese. Patient endurance.

No-self – A central early Buddhist understanding that beings do not have separate, enduring, unconditioned, or permanent properties. It does not mean that beings don't exist.

No Mind – Japanese. Mushin

Okinawa – The main island of the Ryukyu archipelago between mainland Japan and Taiwan. A vassal state of China until the late 19th C. The source of karate.

Path – Used to mean a way in general, a series of stages of development, and a state of mind cultivated at a specific stage of training. Chinese Tao, Japanese Dō.

Path of seeing – The third of the heart Sutra stages of enlightenment, equivalent to Stream Entry and Kensho, the first direct perception of the truth and the threshold of liberation.

Phase transformation – Changes in the properties of a material resulting from changes in their conditions. For example, gradual changes in heat and pressure will abruptly change the properties of water, to ice or to steam for example, as phase transition boundaries – the freezing point or the boiling point – are passed.

Pickelhaube – German. A spiked helmet worn by the Prussian military in the 19th C.

Pinan – A series of five training kata created at the turn of the 20th C. The word means peaceful and safe.

Prajna – Sanskrit. The understanding of the true nature of reality. Translated as wisdom, knowledge or understanding. It is specifically the correct understanding of impermanence, unsatisfactoriness, and no-self nature.

Prajna paramita – The perfection of wisdom.

Renzoku – Continuous movement, flow.

Rinzai – one of the main schools of Japanese Zen, using koan practice, derived from the teaching of Chinese master Lin Chi.

Roshi – Japanese. A senior Zen teacher, a Zen elder, an Abbot.

Ryukyu Kingdom – The monarchy that ruled the Ryukyu Islands as a Chinese tributary state until the Japanese takeover in the late 19th C.

Samatha – Sanskrit. The meditative cultivation of tranquil concentration.

Samyutta Nikaya – Pali. The early Buddhist canonical collection also called the Connected Discourses.

Sati – Mindfulness

Satori – Japanese. Complete enlightenment.

Sen no sen – Japanese. The ability to sense what your opponent is about to do, so you can pre-empt or thwart his intention.

Shako – 18th C. European military headgear. A stovepipe hat with a little brim and decorations.

Shariputra – Chief disciple of the Buddha. Foremost in wisdom. Mahayana sutras like the Heart Sutra and the Vimalakirti give him a hard time.

Shodo – The way of the pen. The art of Japanese calligraphy.

Shorin Ryu karate - Shaolin style. Along with Goju Ryu and Uechi Ryu one of the three main streams of Okinawan karate. Yamabayashi Ryu is a Shorin Ryu style.

Shureido – Okinawan manufacturer and retailer of karate supplies, traditional weapons, belts and uniforms.

Sotapanna – Pali. Stream enterer. A practitioner who has seen the truth, reached the first stage of liberation, passed the threshold of worldly ignorance and is destined to be released from samsara to nirvana.

Soto – Japanese. The largest of the traditional schools of Zen. It emphasizes objectless meditation or shikantaza – just sitting.

STEM – Science, Technology, Engineering and Medicine.

Tantra – Secret or esoteric religious practices using systems of symbols and rituals.

Tao – Chinese. Way, Dō, Path

Te – Japanese. Hand. The name of the indigenous Okinawan fighting method that preceded the development of modern karate in the 20th C.

Theravada – The School of the Elders. The early Buddhist Pali tradition preserved in Sri Lanka and across southern Asia.

Three Marks – the nature of reality, observed in intellectual analysis and perceived deep meditation, is said to be characterized by impermanence, unsatisfactoriness or suffering, and no-self nature. These three marks are generally overlooked.

True nature – Or true reality. Different traditions define this in different ways. Among them are the three marks, sunyata, and the four noble truths.

Vajracchedika Prajna Paramita Sutra – Diamond Cutter Sutra – An influential 9th C. Mahayana sutra.

Vajrayana – Sanskrit. Diamond Vehicle, the esoteric or tantric tradition which flourished in Tibet and spread east.

Vipassana – Insight meditation. It is used by different mediation groups to mean different things. The early meaning pointed to the practices that would yield liberation from the cycle of birth and death in nirvana. The practices focused on the direct perception of the three marks in all phenomena: impermanence, unsatisfactoriness and no-self nature.

Visuddhimagga – Pali. The Path of Purification. By Buddhaghosa. A 5th C. Sri Lankan commentary and compendium of the Buddhist path to enlightenment.

Wu-hsing – A well-known symbol system using five phases in relationship to describe changes in the natural world and inner life. The phases are called Water, Fire, Metal, Wood and Earth.

Yamabayashi Ryu – Mountain Forest Style karate. Which is based on the application of advanced body mechanics, energy flow, and innovation in technical and tactical analysis to practical self-defense, the development of virtue and insight

Yoi – Japanese. Ready. The posture of mind and body at the beginning and end of a karate kata.

Zazen – Japanese. Seated meditation. Especially seated Zen meditation.

Zen – Japanese. Meditation schools.

Zendo – Japanese. A meditation hall.

Author Bio

Jeffrey Brooks has practiced Okinawan karate for more than 40 years. He studied in Okinawa and the US. He has shared karate with thousands of people at his dojo and seminars.

Following graduate school at NYU's Tisch School of the Arts he worked as a writer for prominent public figures, influencers and leaders.

He had a 20-year career in law enforcement, as a patrol officer, an instructor of armed and unarmed combatives, and a detective, working violent, property and sex crimes.

He has trained and studied extensively with scholar-practitioners of western and east Asian religious traditions.

He has focused throughout his career on the exploration of karate kata, their underlying training functions and combative applications;

the unification of body, mind and will through martial arts; the development of concentration and insight through martial arts; and on how to offer people an experience which is healthy, meaningful and good.

Jeffrcy Brooks has written hundreds of published articles and several books about martial arts. He teaches Yamabayashi Ryu karate in western North Carolina, USA.

True Karate Dō, Copyright © 2009 – 2023 Jeffrey M. Brooks

www.ingramcontent.com/pod-product-compliance
Lightning Source LLC
Chambersburg PA
CBHW072037160426
43197CB00014B/2532